ARGYLE PARK

A MEMOIR OF MY SISTER'S SUICIDE

BY

LORNIE WALKER

For Connie & Kit —
At last, the
finished product!
You're next, Connie!
With much love!
Lornie
9/15/06

TRAFFORD

• Canada • UK • Ireland • USA •

Cover image from original watercolor painting by Jacquelyn Lown
Cover design by Paul Wilkin, GargoyleDesign.com

Note for Librarians: A cataloguing record for this book is available from Library and Archives Canada at www.collectionscanada.ca/amicus/index-e.html
ISBN 1-4120-8573-X

Printed in Victoria, BC, Canada. Printed on paper with minimum 30% recycled fibre. Trafford's print shop runs on "green energy" from solar, wind and other environmentally-friendly power sources.

Offices in Canada, USA, Ireland and UK
This book was published *on-demand* in cooperation with Trafford Publishing. On-demand publishing is a unique process and service of making a book available for retail sale to the public taking advantage of on-demand manufacturing and Internet marketing. On-demand publishing includes promotions, retail sales, manufacturing, order fulfilment, accounting and collecting royalties on behalf of the author.

Book sales for North America and international:
Trafford Publishing, 6E–2333 Government St.,
Victoria, BC v8t 4p4 CANADA
phone 250 383 6864 (toll-free 1 888 232 4444)
fax 250 383 6804; email to orders@trafford.com
Book sales in Europe:
Trafford Publishing (uk) Limited, 9 Park End Street, 2nd Floor
Oxford, UK oxi 1hh UNITED KINGDOM
phone 44 (0)1865 722 113 (local rate 0845 230 9601)
facsimile 44 (0)1865 722 868; info.uk@trafford.com
Order online at:
trafford.com/06-0329

10 9 8 7 6 5 4

10% of book sales will be donated
to suicide related programs

Argyle Park is dedicated
to my parents
Lorna and Bill
who did their best in raising us
&
to all parents
especially those who have lost a child to suicide

CONTENTS

ACKNOWLEDGMENTS

I AM deeply grateful to the many friends and family members who have held me accountable to the progression of my book and been witnesses to my healing. To name them all is impossible. Special thanks to Shelley Calabrese, Susan Hesselgrave, Lesley Reed and Ruth Richstad for their long hours of editorial work. I also wish to thank Jacqui Lown for so willingly offering her exquisite original watercolor for the cover. Paul Wilkin of GargoyleDesign.com spent hours illustrating the many different ways he could make the cover design work well, for which I'm extremely grateful.

A few of the members from my various writer's groups have encouraged my writing throughout all or most of the process: Jim Bennett, Hunter Davis, Lesley Reed and Marianne Twyman. Others I wish to acknowledge for providing important feedback and support are Al Ross-Weston, Karla Serapiglia, Noel Symons, Cabby and Hyde Tennis, Pauline Todd, Debra Vaughn and my dear friend Jake Lehrer who died several years ago.

I couldn't have continued on this journey if it weren't for my family, Maggie, Lobo, Alex, Jamie and Tom who tolerated my ups and downs throughout this project. Heartfelt thanks to my husband Tom for standing by me and supporting my hopes and dreams.

AUTHOR'S NOTE

THIS MEMOIR is non-fiction. Although the family at its center is drawn from real life, some of the characters' names have been changed out of respect for their privacy.

INTRODUCTION

I N THE face of my sister's suicide, I struggled for many years with my own depression. For years I tried to understand my sister Mary's life and death and how my life adversely affected hers. But it wasn't until after Mom had died and I was planning to head west again that I began taking a closer look at our family and started to see our relationships in a new way. It was only because Mom was gone that underlying patterns began to surface. She had been the glue in our family, the one who held us all together. With her gone, there was no one to cover up Dad's depression or keep my emotions at bay. I learned more about myself and the unhealthy way I had been holding onto pain, like Dad. The week of May 19, 1994, in Buffalo, became my turning point. I became determined to face my guilt and learn how to rise above my depression. A week-long visit to say good-bye to my dad brought it all home.

I wrote this memoir as my story, a story of a suicide survivor and how it affects those of us left behind. There are numerous ways people experience grief. For me, it was not being able to talk about the suicide which became so crippling. The taboo surrounding suicide is still present, making it difficult for survivors to discuss their feelings openly. I want to share what it has been like to carry guilt and offer up my struggles in hopes of reaching others who may be in similar situations.

Everyone has curve balls thrown at them during their life time. My first and sharpest curve was at birth. I was born 15 months after my sister. She was adopted. I wasn't. Throughout our lives, Mary envied my status as a birth child. I, in turn, strove for the beauty and intellect she possessed. For years Mary would throw accusations at Mom and Dad that they loved me more because I was their birth child. Consequently I was a goody-goody, trying to prove to Mary that my love from our parents was earned, and not due simply to my birth status. This dichotomy became a life-long struggle for us both. The term "primal wound" is used for those who have been adopted and are traumatized by being given away at birth. For Mary, it seemed she was never able to transcend the mystery of her "primal wound."

My story is two-fold. I also delve into the difficulties of coping with aging parents. Brought on by my anticipated long-distance move, I begin to face the emotionally frozen man my father has become. The week-long visit with my father coincides with the anniversary of Mary's suicide, generating flash backs to the years of 1968 through 1977 and the tumultuous experiences that happened in our lives, including Vietnam protests and drug problems.

Drawing upon the spirituality instilled by my mother and my own inner strength, I have discovered healthy ways to move beyond my struggles. Written with compassion and the utmost respect for each character, it is my hope that *Argyle Park* will leave the reader with hope and insights on forgiveness and reconciliation.

ARGYLE PARK

ONE

The Roanoke Street Bridge

Seattle, 1975

"WHAT APPEARS to be an attempted suicide occurred earlier this afternoon when a young woman jumped off the Roanoke Street Bridge," the radio announcer began his top story. "Mary O'Neill... critical condition... Harborview Medical Center." Those words threw me into a harsh reality. The announcer gave more details, but I didn't hear them. My boyfriend Rusty was in mid-sentence, talking with our friend Bonnie who was riding in the back seat. They hadn't heard anything.

It was the spring of '75, the spring I turned twenty-five. I was riding shotgun in my old mustard-colored VW bug. Rusty was driving. We were heading home from a Cesar Chavez rally at the University of Washington. It was from the car radio that I learned my sister was still determined to end her life.

I yelled at them, "That's Mary, that's Mary! She jumped off the bridge!" I could visualize that bridge. I knew it well. We were within minutes of it. It's a bridge that goes over four lanes of Interstate 5 scarcely south of Seattle's University District. We were entering the

1

interstate north of the Roanoke Street Bridge at that very moment. Cars whizzed by as Rusty stayed in the right-hand lane, in disbelief.

"We've got to turn around!" I can still hear the panic in my voice. Rusty pulled off at the next exit, made a u-turn and headed in the direction of Harborview.

On some level, I realized I couldn't face Mary alone, probably fearful of what I might say. Instinct enabled me to direct Rusty to the home of Cabell Tennis who, at the time, was the Dean of Seattle's St. Mark's Cathedral. Cabby, as we called him, was a long-time family friend from Buffalo, NY who had visited Mary a few times during that year. He would be the one person I could turn to. I needed an adult. Ironically I was depending on someone from the very place I was trying to leave behind.

Cabby wasn't home. It was his daughter who answered the door of their stately home on Capitol Hill. I searched for words. He had two daughters, both of whom I had known as kids. To this day, I cannot remember which one listened to my distraught rambling message. Whoever it was assured me she would leave word for her dad about Mary.

The drive to Harborview from their home was a blur. I was tearing apart inside and barely breathing when I ran into the emergency room's information counter seeking the life status of my sister. No one was at the counter, but a few employees were mingling in the background.

"Excuse me." I got the attention of one of the young women. "I just heard on the radio that my sister was brought in here. Mary O'Neill?"

"Yes ma'am." She was matter of fact. "She's stable, but unconscious and being treated for serious burns."

"Burns? What do you mean? I thought she jumped off the bridge." I was totally confused.

"She apparently stuffed newspaper up a leg of her jeans and set herself on fire before the jump. She's in critical condition and no one is allowed to see her."

"I'm her sister," thinking I was more than "no one." "Can't *I* even go in there?"

"Not now, ma'am."

I hated her formality. My concern turned to anger. I was furious at them for releasing her name to the radio station. "What's the deal announcing my sister's name on the radio? Have my parents been notified?"

"I don't know."

"What do you mean you don't know? Who's responsible for notifying the radio?"

"The police are. They release their report to us." She had no sympathy for me.

"Can I see the report?"

"You'll have to contact the police directly." No apology, nothing.

Rusty appeared by my side. "What've you found out?"

"They won't let me see her." I told him the details.

We waited awhile with no encouraging news. I tried clarifying what "critical condition" meant. It was the burns that made her condition extremely serious.

I kept stewing about the insensitivity of the news report. I'm sure the news media didn't care. I imagine the doom and gloom of suicide attempts can make for attractive headlines for our society's sick sense of entertainment.

It was a sunny spring afternoon when Mary jumped into the northbound lanes of I-5, Puget Sound's north-south lifeline. A dark cloud once again loomed above me as I continued to accumulate Mary's burdens.

I was relieved that afternoon when I didn't have to face her. It gave me plenty of time to think. Actually, I probably got stoned with Rusty and forced myself not to think.

The next morning I returned to the hospital to visit Mary. I couldn't do it alone, though, and met Cabby in the lobby of Harborview.

Cabby greeted me with a warm hug and asked how I was doing.

"OK, I guess, but I have no idea what to say. Will you speak to her first?"

"Of course."

I followed him as he spoke with a nurse who led us down a hall. Mary was in some sort of holding room before being admitted to the Burn Unit. It was a large room with several beds, all empty except for Mary's. The sun was shining brightly through the windows, almost surreal.

Mary was lying on her back with her eyes closed. The nurse turned and left us alone.

Cabby spoke. "Mary?"

She opened her eyes and stared at both of us.

"Mary," Cabby began slowly. "Lornie asked me to come with her today. She doesn't know how to respond."

Mary continued to stare.

Looking over Cabby's shoulder, I said, "I love you" and began crying.

A continued stare.

Cabby tried prodding her to speak. "Can you talk?"

"I don't know what to say," she forced softly.

"That's OK, I don't either," I offered between my tears.

She closed her eyes again.

"Would you like us to leave you alone?" Cabby asked Mary.

A simple nod.

"Alright. I'll be back soon," I said.

No response.

∞

Mary survived that jump. Survived. She was alive, but had lost so much. The outward beauty and poise that she had once possessed, were gone. After lying in the burn unit for eight weeks, her face and body were swollen from medications and weight gain. She was scarred from a major cut on her face and skin grafting over much of her body. The bleach had grown out of her shiny golden-streaked hair. Scraggly, dull, brown hair accentuated her long sullen face.

Neither Mom nor Dad came to Seattle during Mary's traumatic ordeal in the burn unit. They kept in touch via telephone, and I never questioned why they didn't come. Maybe the doctors told them it wouldn't be a good idea. Looking back I imagine they didn't know what they could do. But, I also imagine it was their absence that made me feel more responsible. It was only later that I began processing Mary's horrific jump.

TWO

Leaving Again
Buffalo, 1994

JACQUELINE KENNEDY Onassis died on May 19, 1994, the day I
arrived in Buffalo. The memories from that day are just as haunting for me as when John F. Kennedy died. I remember exactly where
I was and what I was doing.

My sister Mary died May 19, 1977, 17 years to the day before
Jackie. Mary and Jackie were strikingly similar. And now they even
shared the same death date. On the day Jackie died, Mary's death
was the furthest thing from my mind. I had just arrived in Buffalo
and, although I didn't know it then, was heading into one of the
most emotional weeks of my life.

I thought I had planned the trip well. For the first time since
Mom died, I'd be going to Buffalo to visit Dad without my husband
and kids. Part of the idea seemed wonderful, almost like a vacation
—no kids for seven days. Heaven! But the more I thought about the
reality of being around Dad and in Buffalo for seven straight days,
the more apprehensive I became.

The week-long visit would be more than a spring vacation from the boys. Our whole family was preparing to move from Syracuse, New York, back to Seattle, Washington. Syracuse was only three hours from Dad. But soon we'd be 3,000 miles out of reach. I wanted to pull at Dad's heartstrings—to make a deep-rooted connection I hadn't felt since childhood. I used to be such a bright light in his life, his precious little girl.

But the older I became, the harder it was to connect with him emotionally, and even more so since Mom died. I never thought Dad would outlive her, or survive those four years since her death. He still smoked his pipe, hadn't taken a walk in years, and spent much of his time in front of the television.

I was angry that Mom was the one who died first. I'm not sure if I was angry at Mom, angry at Dad, or maybe angry at God. To think of Mom as gone made me heartsick. She always took such good care of herself—drank herbal teas, exercised regularly, was an avid reader, and took time out for spiritual reflection.

Mom was at the helm of our family. She was tall, slightly overweight and carried herself well. Her professionally permed, silvery blonde hair was well maintained. Mom had a strong presence when she entered a room. I can hear her now. "Let's get the show on the road." And what a show she could run—luncheons, dinners, cocktail and beach parties. And did Mom know how to mix the right social groups! She was a politician in her own right. She knew how to tell stories, too. I'd give anything to be able to spin a tale and deliver a punch line like she could.

Before Mom died, I had visions of the two of us traveling together. I could see us taking cruises, roaming through Europe, and exploring the world. But with Dad, there weren't any such dreams. Unlike Mom, who loved to travel and knew how to have a good time, Dad sat around, clinging tightly to his money with little desire to do anything.

Buffalo itself had its own stigma for me. Except for a brief two year period when I was first married, I had kept my distance from Buffalo and the small circle of society in which I was raised. The prestigious segregated clubs, the ballroom dances, and the living off of old money all represented values from which I had distanced myself. This extended visit meant I'd have to face those issues in addition to facing Dad.

Mary and I were fortunate to have gone to private schools. From 3rd through 12th grade I went to Park, a country day school. Located on 12 acres with picturesque old wooden bungalows, Park offered science projects surrounding the school's pond, outdoor core classes and numerous hands-on activities. Art-stained pants and dirty hands were part of my everyday experience. I never felt comfortable with the formal, refined facet of my childhood. With buck teeth, gangly legs and cropped blonde hair, I was a tomboy expected to fit into a world of Pappagallo shoes, Lily dresses and cable knit sweaters. Mary had gone to Park for her middle school years, then transferred to an elite all-girls' high school. My values were a far cry from the mirror conscious world Mary at one time enjoyed, the world which eventually would lead her to frustration and unhappiness.

For years I had put the angry yelling fights between Mary and Dad out of my mind. Memories of nights Mary would run to Mom for solace were deeply buried. I was a year younger than Mary and didn't understand what her adolescent fights were about. I built an invisible shell around myself, deciding that if I obeyed Mom and Dad, the anger and conflicts would go away.

∽

ON THE night before going to Buffalo, I was in my bedroom packing my bags when my son Jamie began pestering me.

"I wanna go too, Mom." Jamie said over and over in his whiniest voice. But this trip had been planned solely for me. No way was I was going to let Jamie go, too. He acted more like a two year old than the nine year old he was. I chose not to argue with him. I needed all the energy I could muster to deal with my upcoming visit with Dad. I would have many years to work out my relationship with Jamie. With Dad, my time could be short. He was almost eighty-three.

Jamie didn't want to give it up. "Why can't I go?"

That's when my husband Tom appeared, apparently in an attempt to re-direct Jamie's annoying pestering. "Honey, you're going to need to line up other plans so you won't feel trapped," Tom suggested. He was always trying to protect me. He knew that Dad had probably spread the word that I was coming to town and that Mom's old circle of lady friends would want to take me out to lunch to the exclusive places I had grown to detest.

"OK, OK," I reassured him, "I'll try to have an escape plan."

That night I took Tom's advice and called Karla. Karla was the one friend in Buffalo I could relate with. I had met her during the brief two years Tom and I lived in Buffalo. Karla and I were teachers and developed a kinship based on our genuine love for kids, life and each other. Karla knew of my distaste for Buffalo society, sympathized about my relationship with Dad, and had heard a little bit about Mary. Most importantly, she truly cared about me and I, her.

∞

THE NEXT morning I was up with the sun, ready to hit the road as soon as Tom and I got the boys off to school. Alex, our six-year-old son, was ready to part easily, and Jamie had let go of his push to go with me. I felt upbeat and ready to make this trip with a positive attitude, even though I hadn't been able to let go of my expectations.

After kisses and hugs to Tom and the boys, I threw my bags into the back seat of my '88 maroon Mazda sedan and headed for the New York State Thruway. The drive to Buffalo would take only two and a half hours—a perfect amount of time for reflection and anticipation.

In the car, my mind began focusing on Dad. The image of the tall handsome father I once knew was fading. The distinguished looking, pipe smoking man with dark bushy eyebrows and gray hair was long gone. He now was hunched over, walked with a shuffle and had lost the sparkle in his eyes that Mom's bright presence would evoke. Now, unlike the lively luncheons, bridge and cocktail parties Dad once attended with Mom, his routine consisted of daily trips to church, the bank and the post office. Raised as Episcopalians, our family had always taken an active role within church ministry. And now, since Mom died, Dad's connection with his church had become his main source for personal contact. My arrival would break into his routine. I wondered if he'd take the risk of really acknowledging me. For several years I had been wondering why he was keeping me at arm's length. And even as I entered his world that week of May, 1994, I still struggled with the notion that something must be horribly wrong with me to feel such rejection, to take his lack of eye contact so personally.

I kept trying to imagine how Dad was feeling, knowing I would be moving so far away. Leaving again. I had left before, but that was 1973. Mom and Mary were still alive, and Dad was in excellent health. Mom and Dad probably thought I wouldn't stay out west forever and that the trip that summer of '73 was something I needed to do to get out of my system. They were right to an extent. After ten years out west, I came back, married, settled down and bore two children. But now Mom and Mary were gone, Dad was aging rapidly, and this time I wasn't coming back. I was forty-four. I wasn't a young hippie trying to see what was on the other side of the country. I knew what was there and wanted to make the move permanent.

THREE

Argyle Park

1950s

I<small>T WASN'T</small> long after I left Syracuse and was traveling west on the New York State Thruway that my mind began drifting into the past. I thought back to the place of my childhood.

19 Argyle Park was home for my first eighteen years. A large three-story house in the city—not pretentious, or among the huge estate homes—but, with three-and-a-quarter baths, two fireplaces, a formal dining room and a butler's pantry, most people would consider it large. Argyle Park was one short block set off at each end by unusually large stone walls. A favorite climbing place for children, the walls offered a stately entrance to this sanctuary-like street tucked away in the middle of Buffalo, New York.

Argyle Park was made up mainly of white Protestant families, with the exception of the Rosens who were Jewish. One's religious background has never been an issue for me, but in the community where I was raised, most people didn't stray from their own religious affiliation. Protestants didn't marry Roman Catholics, Catholics didn't marry Jews, and God forbid a white person would marry someone of color.

The Rileys, the Crapes and "mean old Mr. Merry" lived to the south of us. To the north were "old Mr. Gorman," "the widow Wilkes," the Matthews, the Strykers and six other families. There were twenty-six homes in all, twenty-six families who knew each other well. Narrow driveways with detached garages were all that separated us from one another's large homes. We were a close-knit community, sharing parties for Halloween, Christmas, birthdays, cocktails and sometimes afternoon teas for the ladies.

My favorite gathering was the annual Argyle Park carol sing. Everyone would congregate in front of our house or the Franklins' as the children distributed song books. I would sing my heart out, regardless of Mom, who always reminded me that I couldn't carry a tune. In the dark, I felt no one could tell whether I was off-key. Homeowners would light candles in their front windows to greet us as we sang in front of each house. At least one family member would stay home so there would be someone in the window to appreciate the singing. Even the Rosens lit candles and enjoyed the warm sense of community with their neighbors.

Ours was one of the few homes with a prominent front sun room. This, my favorite room, we called the sun porch. An enclosed room overlooking the street, it was built on top of a tall stone wall foundation, flanked on three sides by huge windows—the old-fashioned kind with small panes. Even through the thick, wavy glass we could watch the whole world go by. Once Dad retired, he spent endless hours in this room, watching TV and keeping track of the neighbors. I think it was Mr. Rosen whom Dad had the most fun watching. "Larry must have slept in again today," I can hear Dad saying, as he watched Mr. Rosen walk out to his car across the street, long after the other neighbors had gone to work!

In the early fifties, Mom and Dad put their first TV in the sun porch. I remember Mom telling me that whether or not to purchase the television had been the biggest issue early in their marriage. She was dead set against it. Dad thought it was great. Mom felt it could take over our lives, but Dad won out. With the rabbit ears spread wide on top of the screen, Dad watched the news in the evening and sports on the weekends. Gradually Mom began to join him during the news. A few other shows became acceptable: "Lawrence Welk," "The Carol Burnett Show" and "What's My Line." For us kids, it was "Captain Kangaroo" before school and "Highway Patrol" while Mom was preparing dinner. Mom and Dad gradually let us watch more programs. "The Twilight Zone" and "I Love Lucy" became two of my family's favorite shows. By the time I was a teenager, Mom and Dad had purchased a second TV for their bedroom. And by the time I went to college, they had a third one, small, but still very present on top of the refrigerator. TV had taken over. Mom was right.

Our short, quaint street was lined with huge old elm trees forming an archway. There was a carefully manicured center strip adding to the English charm of the neighborhood. John, the yard man, was hired by the Argyle Park Association to keep the center strip weeded and blooming with flowers. Several households hired John to manage their own yards. Not us. Not until Dad was too old. While Dad was still physically fit, probably well into his sixties, he kept up with the yard work. He and I had special times alone when he'd mow and I'd rake, which didn't take long. Our yards were barely large enough to accommodate a slide and swing set.

The street became our playground. Dad spent endless hours helping me learn to ride a two-wheeler. I held on to the handlebars for dear life as my bike wobbled back and forth down the street. With one hand on the back of the seat, the other on a handlebar, Dad would run along beside me. Again and again, he would hold on until I could find my own balance. Before a devastating elm disease destroyed our beautiful archway of giants, those gorgeous old Dutch elms offered us endless hours of pleasure. Every fall we raked leaves onto the center strip, making the greatest piles, even forts, out of nature's gift, tossing them, hiding and jumping in them until there were no more piles. We'd rake them up again and again, until our bodies itched from the broken leaves and twigs which clung to our hair and clothes. What an idyllic childhood, before Vietnam, before drugs, before we knew how precious our little lives were.

∽

NOLIE STRYKER was the first of us to learn about death. She was my sister Mary's closest friend, and was only eight when her mother overdosed on sleeping pills. No one told her that her mother's death was a suicide, and I'm not sure how many neighbors really knew the truth. But since Argyle was so intimate, I imagine most of the adults knew how Nolie's mom died.

I'm thankful no one told Nolie then how her mom died. Nolie was young and had to quickly learn to deal with a stepmother. Noel, Nolie's Dad, married Gertrude, their housekeeper, within a year of his wife's suicide. I remember Mom telling me that although Nolie had a hard time accepting Gertrude, Noel really needed someone to help parent his children.

As Nolie became a teenager, her fights with Gertrude increased, and her dad struggled with his own inability to be a strong parent. Noel, Mr. Stryker to us kids, was an attorney who worked long, hard hours, spending much of his weekend in their smoke-filled kitchen. I can see him sitting at their kitchen table in his undershirt, sipping coffee and dousing cigarettes. For endless hours he'd let us have the run of his house. Our favorite place was their basement recreation room. Before we were old enough to shoot pool with Nolie's older brother, we played hide and seek behind their huge furnace and made up games pretending we were the invincible Zorro. We arranged Halloween parties for the neighborhood. I remember turning their playroom into a spook house with touchy-feely objects in the dark. The best was a box with a hole cut into it where you were supposed to reach your hand. To the unaware, cold wet spaghetti noodles felt like worms. I can still remember that gross sensation. Gross, yet fun memories I'll treasure forever. But once Noel died, Gertrude wouldn't stand for such ruckus and our fun days at the Stryker's came to an end.

I don't remember the death of Nolie's mother at all. I was six then. But at fourteen, I vividly remember the day Nolie's father died.

It was a Saturday. I learned a new word that day. Mom and I were putting fresh sheets on the four-poster bed. Dad was nearby and answered the phone when Gertrude called.

He hung up telling us he had to go to the Stryker's.

"Gertrude's in a predicament," he said, rushing down the stairs. Mom followed.

I leaned over the banister trying to hear their conversation. Her face was stricken as she came back upstairs and told me, "Noel, I mean Mr. Stryker, is having trouble breathing."

I didn't understand, but knew something horrible was happening and asked Mom, "What's 'predicament' mean?"

"It's when someone has a problem and they're not sure what to do." Mom explained.

It seemed merely minutes after Dad had left that the phone rang. "Oh no!" Mom exclaimed.

I was sitting next to her on their bed trying to hear the other end as Mom listened. "Who is it? What's wrong?" I nagged.

"Just a second," she said into the phone. She covered the mouth piece with her hand as she looked at me and said, "It's Dad. Mr. Stryker has died. Now be quiet, I've got to listen."

I sat there desperately trying to hear Dad on the other end, but all I could hear was something about more phone calls.

Predicament, I thought. It seemed like Gertrude was in more than a predicament.

Nolie and Mary drove up our driveway soon after Dad called. They were returning from Bergers, a locally owned department store, the small one that catered to the upper-class. On the day Mr. Stryker died, Mary and Nolie had been shopping for specialty bras. Mary was a few months older than Nolie and had just passed her driver's test. She was excited to be driving and had a smile on her face as she drove up our driveway.

I was at the side door following Mom who was carrying the awful news she needed to share with Nolie. The screen door almost slammed in my face as I tried to get as close to the action as possible. I felt sorry for Mom and wondered how she was going to tell Nolie.

Not taking the time to put the car in the garage, Mary parked it in the middle of the driveway.

With her gorgeous high cheekbones, captivating hazel eyes, long golden-streaked hair and usual flair, she hopped out of the driver's seat and flew around the front of the car, swinging her bra bag. She held it up high, proudly for Mom to see. Nolie got out of the passenger side looking a little embarrassed as Mary boasted, "Wait 'til you see our new bras!"

Mom couldn't do it. She looked at Nolie and told her, "Something has happened to your Dad and you need to get home right away." She didn't lie. I imagine she just didn't want to be the one to tell Nolie the horrible news.

"What happened?"

I could feel my heart beat as I wondered what Mom might say. I couldn't imagine how she would break the news about Nolie's namesake. I had never been this close to someone's death.

Mom paused, then repeated, "You just need to get home right away."

I pushed the screen door open, joined Mary and Mom at the end of our driveway, and watched as Nolie walked past the three houses that separated us, to her front door.

Mom turned to Mary, "Mr. Stryker died. Dad's down there with Gertrude now."

"I can't believe it."

"None of us can," Mom replied. "Poor Nolie. Having to lose both parents when you're young will be hard," she said knowingly.

The three of us went into the house. We followed each other out to the sun porch, probably thinking we could see some answers from there. We stood looking down the street toward the Stryker's waiting for Dad to come home.

It seemed to take Dad forever. Mom told Mary and me that there are a lot of arrangements that have to be made when someone dies. And she presumed that Gertrude had given Dad many responsibilities.

When Dad finally came home, he joined us in the sun porch. "When I first told Nolie that her father had died, she couldn't believe it and started to cry." Dad paused, taking a deep breath. "Nolie wanted to see him, but Gertrude didn't think it was a good idea. She told Nolie that she was a big girl now and not to cry."

Dad told us about what I believe must have been one of his most courageous and empathetic moments. He walked Nolie past Gertrude and up the stairs to the bedroom, where only an hour earlier Nolie's father seemed to have been napping. Dad told her to go ahead and cry her heart out.

Death became a regular resident of Argyle Park. The Strykers were both gone and old Mr. Gorman, who lived next door, had died. But it was the strange coincidence of all of Argyle's suicides that made me really wonder how our quaint little street, only one block long, could have such a presence of tragic deaths.

The Youngs, a family of five, moved in next door after the elderly Merrys died. Mr. Young took his life when he was thirty-something. I had gone off to college and didn't know their family well, but was affected by Mom and Dad's sadness. They had developed a close relationship with the Youngs. All that came between our dining room window and theirs was a tiny strip of grass and low cut bushes. As we had with the Merrys, we watched them eat, and they us. Mom and Dad had become surrogate grandparents to their three young children and were heart broken when they learned Mr. Young had committed suicide. He jumped out of his office window on an upper floor of a downtown building. During my first visit back to Buffalo after Mr. Young died, I remember lying awake in my old bedroom, merely a few yards from his bedroom. I wondered why someone couldn't have stopped him, how his life could have been so terrible that he would want it to end. I don't remember Mom or Dad talking much about his death, except to say that he must have had problems we didn't know about.

And there was Bob Nichols, who used to live in the brick house. He was a close friend of Mom's and Dad's who had moved off Argyle and away from Buffalo. Mom and Dad received a letter from Bob's wife telling them he had died. Mom told me he had always struggled with depression, had an alcohol problem, and that his death was probably a suicide.

The Argyle Park suicides in the fifties and sixties were sad, and yet still distant enough from my life that their impact didn't adversely affect me. But it was in 1977 that death got hold of me and wouldn't let go. In May of that year, my sister Mary, age twenty-eight, also chose to end her life.

FOUR

Kick-The-Can

During my dark days and years of depression, the frolicking years of Argyle Park became a blur. But that week in May of '94, as I headed toward Buffalo in my dependable Mazda 323, I let Argyle Park come alive for me again.

I KEPT THINKING about those early days on Argyle, the fun days when Mary and I would venture around the block every Saturday to spend our weekly allowance. I must have been eight, Mary nine, when we experienced our first taste of freedom from Mom and Dad. Prindle's Candy Store was just around the corner. The candy was, I'm sure, strategically placed at children's eye level behind a glass counter. From candy cigarettes and Lick-a-Maid, to our favorite, red licorice, old Mr. Prindle would help us whittle our money away.

Our older brother Tommy was a teenager when Mary and I were first checking out our freedom. He spent his allowance on records and radio equipment. Tommy turned our garage roof into an outdoor arena, setting up speakers and providing props. The flat roof was a ready-made stage. It was there his friends were invited to lip-sync Elvis songs. It was the late fifties and early sixties, when Elvis was still fresh and utterly handsome. With guitar in hand, one of my brother's friends, Stan Harrison, would shake his hips and rattle his legs like Elvis, unequaled by any other contender except the King himself.

Pictures of Elvis were plastered on the walls and ceiling of Tommy's third-floor bedroom. He had the entire attic to himself and in the height of puberty, his identity began to change. Like many teenagers, he dropped the "y" and became Tom. What once was a large attic storage room became the indoor stage for Tom's performers. Mary and I were rarely allowed in his sanctuary. But one winter, he invited us to participate in one of his shows. In fact, the whole neighborhood was invited. "Singing in the Rain" was my big hit. Mary had a special role that I'm sure she loved. She stood behind a curtain with a bucket of water and, not so slowly, poured it over my umbrella as I lip-synced that old song!

Tom's always been "the quiet" one in our family. Interacting with Mom or Dad, and even with Mary or me, was low on his priority list. He preferred to hang out on the third floor or with his friends, who took on new names to fit their personality or looks. Tom's friend Billy became "Chin," another friend became "Semo," and Tom became "The Wolf" or "Lobo." His friends thought that, in profile, he looked somewhat like a wolf. Lobo and his buddies wired a forty-block radius for an underground radio station. WAND, "650 on your dial" was broadcast to at least 1,000 households for over two years from Lobo's attic room on Argyle Park. I can hear Lobo now broadcasting the Argyle Radio Corporation (ARC)—"This is the magical WAND station of Buffalo, spreading an arc all over the city."

Lobo and I still recall fond memories of the "rag man." We almost have to pinch ourselves to think we grew up in the days when a horse and cart were still, although infrequently, a part of our world. A little old man, collecting rags, would steer his horse and cart down Argyle, calling out with a cracking voice, "raaaaaaaaags?, raaaaaaaags?"

∞

I REACHED for an apple from the seat beside me, hoping that the snacks I brought would allow me a nonstop drive. As long as I don't have to pee, I thought, laughing out loud. I began doing kegal exercises and thought of my old nickname, "LLLA" for Leaky Lornie Leaks Again. What a legacy! LLLA was the nickname given to me by a bunch of Argyle Park kids when I was seven or eight. I could never hula-hoop or jump rope without losing bladder control. It seemed as though half the neighborhood was yelling, "There goes LLLA, Leaky Lornie Leaks Again!" when I would run down the street headed for home, holding my crotch. I lived with that nickname for many years and wet my pants countless times. I felt ashamed of myself and extremely vulnerable to those kids.

It wasn't just the kids who teased me. I wet my bed for what seemed like forever. Mom, in a teasing voice, would say she'd cure me by college! They tried everything. Every night at Mom and Dad's cocktail hour I had to drink a half cup of green stuff that tasted like water. It was my "Green Water Cocktail." We called it GWC for short. Whether it was the GWC or adjustment into puberty, my bedwetting did subside. And I'm quite certain I stopped wetting before high school. Although, whenever anyone mentioned bedwetting, Mom loved to tell them my saga and laugh about how they "cured" me before college.

But for me, Leaky Lornie was an all too real name. It's hard to imagine shaking that image, especially since I still have difficulty with my bladder capacity. I can laugh about it now, but at the time, it was one more thing which made me feel rejected and inferior to Mary. My insecurities began early. In contrast to Mary, I was not pretty. No one told me I was beautiful.

I was "LLLA," lacking the physical and muscle control Mary always demonstrated. She had style. She carried herself with pride and radiated beauty. She excelled in sports. Not me. I lacked balance and poise.

How could I ever forget the day Mary and I were in a ballet performance. It was in a neighbor's fancy new basement recreation room. At least ten little girls with their pink, white, and frilly tu-tus were dancing all over a well constructed, three-foot high stage. As the music wound down, we spiraled off into a triangular shape, with my graceless self as the front point facing the audience. The music stopped and the rest of the kids left the stage area. I didn't realize they were gone until Mary reappeared from behind and, in an effort to tell me to leave the stage, kicked me in the butt! Of course, I lost my balance and went flying forward. Landing on all fours, slowly lifting my head up to the roar of all the parents and siblings, I felt like a fool.

Some people are natural born klutzes. Born left-handed, I felt cursed. I used to have to stay after school in second grade to practice my "horrible" handwriting. And I was always spilling things. It was almost as if my family expected my clumsiness. Physical balance was not part of my being. But I was able to find balance in other ways. Balance would come for me when I was enjoying nature, when I slowed my pace to appreciate the natural world.

When I was seven on Argyle Park, all I needed was a snowsuit, hat, gloves and a shovel. Buffalo is known for its big snowstorms. One of the things I loved most in the winter was making angels in the freshly fallen snow. Lying on my back, arms straight out from my sides, I would fly. From head to toe, my arms and legs would glide, forming the skirt and wings, until I became one with the angel imprinted in the snow. My mouth opened as naturally as a baby's does waiting for her next spoonful of applesauce. The snowflakes would fall, one after another, wetting my tongue, tickling my nose and forcing my eyes to close. Trying to keep the perfect image of my angel, I would slowly lift myself from the deeply imprinted angel, praying that I could keep that peaceful and beautiful image. Sometimes I could do it perfectly, but other angels were ruined by my infamous clumsiness. I never gave up. I would do it over and over until I felt it was just right.

Nolie, Mary and I and a few others would form snow mazes. Like bunnies, we hopped and stomped our feet through the virgin snow, forming the most intricate trails in our not-so-big back yards. We turned our side yard into a sledding hill. After several sledding trips, we would wear down mean old Mr. Merry's grass, infuriating him. I remember the tension on his face when he came out yelling. We'd disperse quickly, like the bunnies we had become hopping through the trails in the backyard.

Countless times Argyle Park would become impassable. Snowplows dared not enter our narrow street for fear of denting the old Studebakers and Chevys. But the snowbound street didn't dampen our community spirit. Whether it was four inches or four feet, we would be out there shoveling snow off not only the sidewalks and driveways, but also the entire street.

Huge snow piles would form on the center strip from all our shoveling. From there we built the most incredible snow forts, lining up rows upon rows of snowballs, ready to bombard each other. The snowball wars became ferocious. Ice balls were my biggest fear. Being the youngest on the block, I managed to duck out of the wars first. With a sweaty body, rosy cheeks, frozen hands and tears streaming down my face, there was nothing greater than coming into our toasty house for hot chocolate. Mom gave up her futile yelling at the older kids. I was the youngest and would always be their best target. If I chose to play outside with them, she couldn't guarantee my safety. But once in the house, I felt safe.

Our house had a warm feel to it. Mom chose soft colors and floral designs for decorating. Tasteful and probably very expensive, deep pink, floor-length silk drapes accented the intricate tapestry of the Oriental rug in the dining room. The long rectangular dining room table matched the dark mahogany Victorian sideboard, buffet and china cabinet.

The living room was formal, too. Flowered upholstered chairs and a soft, pale blue sofa offered cozy comfort, unlike the living room at the Stryker's. Gertrude had covered their living room furniture with plastic, something I never saw in any other home. Our whole family thought it was weird. Mom wouldn't let us put our feet on the furniture, but compared to the crinkly sound of plastic at Nolie's house, our furniture felt comfortable.

19 Argyle was heated with old steam radiators. In the living room, the waist-high radiators were covered with built-in cases. But in the sun porch, the radiators were tall and uncovered. Mary and I used to boost ourselves up on top, trying not to burn our butts! Sitting high on those old radiators gave us a sense of power. Once as teenagers, Mary had me take photos of her sitting up there posing in stylish hats. Mary idolized Jackie Onassis and tried to emulate her. Very serious, almost mysterious, Mary carried a sophisticated look most of the time, similar to Jackie.

Sliding down the banister, wrestling matches in the front foyer, giving rides on the bathroom rug (pulling each other back and forth) are just a few more of the good memories from 19 Argyle. It seemed to be an easy way of life. Mom stayed home, always there to be our taxi service. We were a typical fifties family. We collected S&H green stamps, had milk delivered in the old glass bottles, and ate Wonder Bread. Dad didn't make much money, but we lived comfortably. Later I found out he received extra financial help from his parents. Deprivation was never part of our vocabulary. I felt secure.

I remember when my sense of security was first challenged. I was about nine or ten when Mom told me I was old enough to sleep without my teddy bear. There was no way she was going to keep me from sleeping with my best buddy. Imagining Mom never knew, I set Teddy on my bedside radiator, tied one end of a string around him, the other around my bedpost, and after Mom said goodnight and closed the door, I pulled Teddy in beside me and felt totally safe and secure.

Strange, how safe and secure I felt as a child. I was raised to believe safety and security were enough. Long after leaving Buffalo I realized that I'd never learned how to deal with emotions. Mom never seemed to allow herself to feel pain. Dad would feel it and not let it go. I would vacillate between painful depression and superficial happiness. But it wasn't until that day, driving to Buffalo, when I flashed back to Argyle Park, that I became determined to deal with my own emotions.

Mary was adopted. I wasn't. Trapped between Lobo, the unobtrusive first child who was also adopted, and me, the young miracle baby who'd displaced her, I believe Mary had a terrible time being the middle child. She struggled with many issues, but her free spirit was always darkened by her inner yearning to seek her birth parents.

At some point in life it seems that someone will always shatter childhood illusions. In our lives, that someone was our neighbor, Debbie Driscoll. She told us there was no Santa and it was she who destroyed the Tooth Fairy myth. She probably instigated the LLLA nickname. Lobo and I can't remember, but imagine it was Debbie Driscoll who prompted seven year old Mary to run home in the middle of one of our kick-the-can games. I didn't hear what was said, but I do remember watching Mary run in the back door and into our kitchen, letting the screen door slam behind her. From the back porch I saw Mom standing at the kitchen sink peeling potatoes. I can still smell the meat loaf baking. Mary blurted to Mom, "You aren't my real mother."

"That's not true," Mom was quick to say. "We told you that we chose you. We brought you home from the hospital. You are our baby, our chosen little girl."

"But I didn't come out of your tummy, right?" Mom looked beyond Mary and saw me standing on the porch and told me she needed to talk to Mary alone. I was only six and unsure of what was happening. I went back out to Argyle's center strip where the kick-the-can game had abruptly come to an end. A neighbor girl whom I barely knew told me that Mary was adopted. I didn't even know what the word adoption meant.

It was after that incident that Mom told me I was the "bonus" baby, that they didn't think they could have children. They adopted Lobo, then Mary, and then the miracle happened. Mom was pregnant with me.

"You love Lornie more than me because she's your own." In front of me, throughout our elementary and adolescent years, Mary would throw accusations at Mom and Dad more often than I care to remember. But I do remember and it still hurts. It was probably then that I began burying my feelings, and deciding I needed to be "the strong one."

I was the "bonus baby." Or so Mom, in my presence, would tell her friends, in an effort to reassure me, I suppose. I was the one they always hoped for, but she couldn't convince me. I never felt like a bonus. Instead, I believed I was the miracle baby that crippled Mary's chance of ever feeling secure. I saw myself as the mistake. I *was* a mistake. Mom and Dad had already adopted two children, the children they had hoped to have naturally, but whom they accepted as part of God's plan. I don't think anyone ever told me, but I feel certain that they never planned on a third child. I feel it was just common sense. They had been told they couldn't have any children and had given up trying. They had a five-year-old son, a fifteen-month-old daughter, and at age thirty-nine, I am certain Mom hadn't planned on another one. She was five months along before her mother convinced her to go to the doctors and have the pregnancy confirmed.

And when Mary threw those "you love Lornie more" stabs at Mom and Dad, Mom would try hard to reassure her. "We chose you," Mom would tell Mary. "We wanted you more than anything."

Mary didn't see it that way. The birth vs. adopting mother issue had begun and Mary's wound was irreversible. For most of her life she wanted to find out who her birth parents were. She needed to know why someone gave her away, why someone else didn't want her more than anything.

Mom and Dad tried not to make a big deal out of it. But for Mary it was a big deal. Mary's ultimate feeling of rejection, I believe, must have been in living with the knowledge that her birth mother gave her away. She felt unwanted and acted on it immediately. I didn't consciously react until years later.

How was it that the neighborhood kids knew our family's origin and we didn't? Reflecting on this now, having heard the truth from others first doesn't make me angry at Mom and Dad. They were doing what they thought was best. But as a child, I couldn't see it that way and spent too many years feeling guilty for being their birth child.

Similar to Mary's deep pain in yearning for her birth mother, I held on to a deep feeling of rejection. I was the baby Mary had to contend with, the one who took the attention away from the toddler who was still wanting. The dichotomy between Mary and me made it impossible for Mom or Dad to meet our emotional needs. Our family became obsessed with trying to make her feel accepted. There wasn't anything Mom wouldn't do for her. Nothing Mom wouldn't buy for her. And there was nothing I could do to become their 'chosen' little girl.

Mom probably felt terribly torn between us. I imagine she felt wounded by Mary's stabbing accusations, no matter how hard she tried to pretend she wasn't. And her fear of showering me with too much affection in front of Mary probably stifled her innate desire to show me love.

⬯

"BUFFALO—24 MILES." The sign jumped out at me as I sped by, stunned that I was almost "home." But my mind kept racing. Why wouldn't Mary let me help her? I thought. Why was I always the bad guy? I would have given anything to have her in the car with me right then. Right beside me so we could make amends. I was married. I had children. I had a better perspective on relationships. And it made me sad to think I didn't have another chance with her. Her loss seemed to compound the other losses I was learning to live with—the loss of Mom, the loss of Dad's ol' self, and the loss of Argyle and the early days, when we would jump in the leaf piles and spend our allowance at Prindle's, the time when driving a car meant you could go bra shopping by yourself. I tried to get a grasp on my thoughts about the past and Argyle Park. Mom and Dad loved, laughed and cried together for forty-five long years on Argyle. But 19 Argyle had a new family now. Lobo and I packed it up the summer Mom died.

FIVE

Stepping into a Foreign World

Buffalo, 1994

My husband Tom had helped me focus on special time for each one of my family members. For Dad it was going to be a night at the movies. As I usually did with Lobo, we would go to Nietzsche's, his favorite bar, to hear music. Maggie, Mary's only child, was twenty-six. For our time together we planned a dinner and an overnight at her new apartment. Since the drive to Buffalo became boggled with flashbacks and anxiety about my reunion with Dad, I was grateful that my week had already been carefully planned; one less worry.

As I watched the familiar exit signs approaching, I tried to visualize Dad's perspective, but couldn't quite conceive it. Many of our aging parents are losing control of their lives, but Dad still had control of his. He still drove, although his declining reflexes were cause for worry. He still paid his own bills. God forbid Dad would ever let anyone else control his money. Part of my anxiety, I realized, was my own fear that he wanted control over my move west.

Dad had never made any negative comments about our move, but I had imagined he didn't want me to leave the East Coast. Maybe, I thought, it was because he had lost Mom and needed someone with a bright spirit. Maybe it was because he was born and raised in Buffalo and wanted to keep the family there. And just maybe it was me, that I wanted him to need me.

Mom had been a domineering factor in Dad's life. She controlled their activities, their way of being. I had some of the same control issues. It seemed important to me to control this visit, but as Maggie had forewarned me, Dad would have control of where we went to dinner that first night. He had chosen to go to the Saturn Club, a place I'd rather not go, a place that evoked all those old feelings about Buffalo's pretentious upper class. But, in an effort to avoid conflict, I reminded myself that it was a unique chance for the four of us, my only remaining kin, to have a quiet evening together.

As I pulled off the New York State Thruway, I headed straight for Argyle Park, momentarily forgetting that the house had been sold and Dad was no longer there. "Argyle Park, Argyle Park," I mumbled to myself. "Put it behind you, take a deep breath." Abruptly I was able to correct my direction and head for Dad's new home, Delaware Towers. He had a condominium on the 14th floor with an incredible view of the city. Within minutes I was in the double-doored foyer waiting to be let into the lobby. I buzzed Dad's room. I could hear him mumbling through the speaker, sounding unsure if the intercom really worked.

I called into it. "Dad, it's me. I'm here."

The door buzzer sounded and I let myself in. The security guard at the front desk recognized me as Mr. Walker's daughter and had just stood up to let me in when Dad and I connected through the intercom. But would we be able to connect in person?

The security guard greeted me warmly with his loving Ethiopian smile and a warm hug. I had become a regular visitor over the past several years. But usually I had the boys with me.

"Where are your boys?" he asked.

"This time I'm alone—a chance to have a special visit with Dad before we move to Seattle."

He looked sad. "Seattle? But that's far away!"

Far away—the issue that had been provoking all my reminiscing thoughts for the past two and a half hours. "I know." I sighed. "It's going to be hard. But I love it out there. I lived there several years ago and I'm ready to return."

"We will miss you," he offered sincerely.

"Me, too." I headed toward the elevator doors. "I'll be here for a week—see you later."

As the elevator approached the 14th floor I could feel my heart beat quicken. The palms of my hands were sweating. I told myself to take a deep breath. The elevator door opened. Yet another deep breath. I headed down the long hallway, ready to make the best of my visit. "Put on a good face," Mom would say.

The door to Dad's apartment was ajar. In the few short minutes since he had buzzed me in, he had unlocked the door and gone back to his chair.

"Hey Dad," I cried out as I walked through the tiny kitchen into the living area. The TV, his lifeline, was blaring as I announced my arrival over the din of CNN's constant news. Dad slowly raised himself from the chair, greeting me with a smile. "Hi, honey," he said, and we gave each other a hug.

It had been only a few months since I had seen him. Only since Christmas. But the change in his appearance was extraordinary. His unshaven face, soiled button-down shirt, and unkempt hair were signs that he hadn't been taking care of himself. It was hard to fathom the tall handsome man Dad had once been. He still had the gray bushy eyebrows I was so fond of, but with no life in his eyes and his head hung low, he had lost his distinguished presence. My sadness in moving far away from Dad deepened. I felt pulled to stay and take care of him, while knowing that was impossible.

As usual upon my arrival almost anywhere, I announced I had to pee. He understood. The guest bathroom was clean, probably not used since my last visit. What a lonely life he must lead here, I thought. Returning to the living room, I intentionally studied his surroundings more thoroughly. There were new burn marks on the carpet from his pipe smoking, with fresh food stains also marring the light gray carpet. His newspapers, magazines and mail were cluttering up every conceivable table space. I couldn't imagine him living on his own much longer.

I knew I needed to turn my thoughts around and put on that "good face" Mom had so deeply ingrained in me. It was a craft both Maggie and I had learned well. For Mary it had been different. There was a fine line between Mary's willingness to conform and her stubbornness to rebel. If it was for beauty's sake, she'd smile pretty. But many times, she'd become obstinate, wearing a stern, somewhat harsh look. For me, who has never liked making waves, I would put on my "good face" to cover any anxiousness and avoid conflict.

I tucked my feelings away and tried to re-enter Dad's world.

"It was a perfect day for driving," I told him.

He mumbled that it was, but he seemed more focused on the TV than my presence. No wonder Mom had fought so hard to keep the TV from entering their lives. Whenever we talked on the phone, even if Dad was calling me, the TV was blaring in the background and he referred to the program while he was supposedly listening to me.

With the TV dominating Dad's attention, I glanced around the sunlit room with its large picture windows overlooking Delaware Avenue and downtown Buffalo. The old familiar photos and paint-

ings captured my attention. Most prominent was the large oil painting of Lake Erie and the Pt. Abino Lighthouse, the view from our
summer home. And on the opposite wall were two framed photos—in one, the serene beauty pose of Mary in the fur cape she
modeled for *Towne and Country*, and in the other, the earthy pose
of me in a knit winter cap on the waterfront of Whidbey Island,
Washington; another striking contrast of our differences.

As my eyes continued to move around the room, I spotted the
newspaper sitting on the tray table next to Dad. "Jacqueline Kennedy Onassis Loses Battle To Cancer," the headline read. I told
Dad that I had heard the priest had given her last rites the previous
night.

We talked a little bit about the former First Lady when I remembered the headlines from my visit earlier that year—"Richard
Millhouse Nixon dead at age 80." I made some sly remark about
heavy headlines whenever I came to Buffalo, but kept staring at the
newspaper date, May 19, 1994. It was as though I had turned away
during a baseball game and was suddenly clobbered in the head by
a ball. It was the anniversary of Mary's death. How could I have not
realized that the anniversary of her death would be the day I arrived
in Buffalo? I had always paid so much attention to that date.

"May 19th, oh my God, Dad. That's the same date Mary died."

He pondered and asked, "Is that right?" with his usual blasé effect. Certainly I couldn't expect him to remember that date. Except
for Maggie, I always had been alone in remembering it year after
year.

I would always call or write Mom and Dad on May 19th, needing support. Mom would tell me she tried hard to forget that awful
day, that there were some things in life you needed to put behind
you and that was one of them. She would tell me we needed to
move on with our lives.

But her ability to put it behind her was much greater than mine.

I finally decided to sit down across from Dad, but there was no way we would be able to visit with the noise of the TV. CNN started recapping Jackie's life. Jackie's death and all of her pictures on TV and in the newspaper started bringing back painful memories of my sister. This was going to be a long week, I thought.

Mary and Jackie were photographed for their beauty and elegance. Equaling Jackie's poise, Mary appeared in *Town and Country* in November, 1971. *Town and Country* had run a special section on Buffalo, featuring our city's most influential families. It was always a mystery to me why they chose someone from our family since we weren't considered part of the rich and elite. And Dad's common job as a comptroller for a small private airport certainly didn't classify him as influential. I imagine it was for Mary's beauty that she was asked to model. She looked stunning in both the luxurious fur jacket and contemporary cape she modeled. Mary and Jackie were debutante queens who held out for the most eligible bachelors. Jackie married Jack, the young handsome politician. Mary married Daniel, a young handsome and probably most sought after bachelor in our small community in Buffalo. Mary, Mary, Mary. I couldn't get her out of my head. I wanted to focus on Dad, but kept allowing my thoughts to trail off.

Thank goodness Maggie would be with us tonight, I thought. She would be the pearl of my visit. She was nine when her mother died and twenty-six now. All these years, Maggie treated me as a surrogate mother, calling me in the middle of the night, pouring her heart out during her tumultuous teenage years, knowing she could put her trust in me.

Maggie was to meet us at The Saturn Club. But shortly after I arrived, she called from work to tell me her van was being repaired and she would need a ride. On the phone we realized we'd have some time alone with each other before dinner. We were psyched.

Just as I hung up, Lobo arrived, with his arms full of groceries. Slowly putting one bag down at a time, he welcomed me with a smile and reached out for a hug. Now I can relax, I thought.

I had made initial contact with everyone. Both Lobo and Dad are easy going with no pretensions themselves, but still, I always hated stepping into the Buffalo world which had become foreign to me.

Lobo looked tired, as though taking care of Dad was starting to wear on him. He was fifty now and had chopped off his long pony tail, making his gray more apparent. His belly was beginning to bulge, a sign, I presumed, of good drinking.

Lobo didn't like the Buffalo social world either, never conforming to that formal part of our lives. I often thought of him with a Peter Pan image, not wanting to grow up. He had taken a long hiatus from Buffalo after Viet Nam. I always figured it was Mary's death that brought him "home." He didn't share his feelings, but I'm certain that it was no coincidence that his first of many returns to Buffalo occurred shortly after Mary's death. Maybe he wanted to let Mom and Dad know they hadn't lost two children.

For many years he and Dad were at odds with each other. When Lobo was in high school, had his own car and was of drinking age, he stayed out 'til all hours of the night (New York State was one of the few places you could drink at age eighteen). Dad would be livid as Lobo tried quietly to come in late at night and head to his third-floor refuge. Dad would drag himself out of bed and, from outside my bedroom door, yell up the attic stairs, demanding that Lobo tell him where the hell he'd been. Lobo ignored Dad's outbursts, just as he ignored our entire family when he moved away after Viet Nam. He moved first to New York City, then to San Francisco. We knew little of his new life, other than he was the sound man for some local rock groups. He had his own life, his own friends and had long since let go of Mom and Dad. They rarely talked about him during those years. Lobo had become invisible.

Maggie, born in 1968 while Lobo was still in Nam, became the light of their lives. Lobo was the thorn, Maggie, the rose. And what a rose she was. Her warm, sensitive being resembled the delicateness of the most perfect rose.

But Lobo came back. After Mary died he visited every summer. Year after year, from San Francisco, he would come to Buffalo. He returned to stay the summer of 1990 when Mom was close to death. Lobo was a godsend when Mom was dying. He fed her every day. For Mom's last two months, he would go to the nursing home with V-8 juice and vitamins and make sure she had some nutrition. I remember how hard it was for him to agree to sign the "do not resuscitate" order for Mom. The mom who gave him loads of love. The one who was proud of him because he had returned.

Lobo's adoption was never an issue for him, like it was for Mary. He believes that both the birth mother and father had a good reason that they couldn't be parents. He did the same thing. During the height of his experimental drug days and irresponsibility, he and a former San Francisco girlfriend gave up for adoption what was to be Lobo's only child, a son. How hard it must be knowing that he has a son out there somewhere in this world. He still lives with it and says it's OK. But, even if it wasn't OK, he wouldn't admit the pain. Similar to Dad, his feelings are deeply repressed. He had worked hard to regain a place within our family. And now he was the prodigal son, making sure Dad was seen through his final days.

Lobo spent many late nights chasing double Skyy vodkas with beer at his favorite bar, Nietzsche's. His days were spent visiting Dad, assisting him with grocery shopping, doctor appointments and cooking a meal here and there. Now he was Dad's godsend.

MAGGIE WAS waiting in front of the family manufacturing business her dad now ran. She had been working there several months, learning computers and public relations. Just as beautiful as her mother, but seemingly with more inner confidence, Maggie walked toward my car. She leaned down into the passenger window and smiled her radiant green-eyed smile as she started opening the door. She looked picture perfect, her long brown hair swept around her face as she climbed in. We hugged and kissed and headed for her apartment so she could change for dinner. As we turned down her street, only two blocks from Argyle Park, I asked if she had heard about Jackie's death. She had. Surprisingly, she hadn't connected the death date, but she did remember the similarities between Mary and Jackie.

With a serious yet flattered look on her face, she said "Just the other day someone asked me if anyone ever told me *I* looked like Jackie Onassis!" I was still driving, but turned to face her for a moment. She too has the same full, dark eyebrows of Mary and Jackie, and high cheek bones that help shape the beauty of her stunning face.

"You do!" I acknowledged. It was at that moment I began wondering aloud. "God, Maggie, maybe you're related to the Bouviers (Jackie's kin). We still have no idea who Mary's birth parents are. Can you imagine?"

She laughed and said it was impossible. Her voice became serious. "I was thinking of starting a search for my mom's birth parents. Do you think that's a good idea?"

"I've always wanted to know who they are," I encouraged her. "It could be a symbolic gift to Mary. Mary always wanted to know so desperately. And anyway, maybe you could find out if you really are related to Jackie Kennedy." I, too, thought it was impossible that Mary could've been a Bouvier, but it was fun to fantasize being related to someone famous.

We talked about what a hard process it is to find birth parents. Maggie had learned that in order to begin the process, she would need a copy of Mary's death certificate. I agreed to follow up on it once we moved to Seattle where Mary had died.

As we traipsed up the three stories to her apartment and art studio, Maggie began to focus on the evening and the birth parent topic was dropped. She decided to take a shower. I used the bathroom before she took it over and noted that, just like Mary, she had tons of lotions, shampoos, hair conditioners and an army of beautifying paraphernalia. Always caught up in appearance, I thought.

∞

THE FOUR of us walked into the Saturn Club ahead of the crowd. Dad always liked to get there early, especially for Friday Night Fish Fry when reservations weren't accepted. I looked around the familiar setting; the tall ceilings, dark mahogany moldings, and heavy turn of the century drapes were all signs of the enclave in which I was raised. Mom had known better than to expect me to go there, but for Dad, I made the extra effort.

Only certain people could join; color, status and wealth played a big part in it. It was a circle of society similar to Argyle Park. There was only one member of color there. And that was because his Mom was white, wealthy and prominent; the father, a mystery.

We were seated by Peter who knew Dad by name.

"Good to see you, Mr. Walker," Peter greeted Dad as he passed around the menus. "Looks like you've got the whole family here."

"Sure do." Dad sounded proud.

With a pleasant smile Peter was off as quickly as he had come.

"He'll return shortly to get our cocktail orders," Dad assured us.

Maggie started right in on her latest relationship. All three of us, Dad, Lobo and I, loved to hear about Maggie and her boyfriends. With a slight giggle, Maggie told us about her longest relationship yet. Her current boyfriend had left Buffalo to go to school in Pittsburgh. The long distance relationship was too one-sided and Maggie was getting tired of it. From Maggie's account, it looked like the end was in sight.

Lobo and Dad just sat there, listening. Lobo has never been much of a conversationalist, so it was easy to let Maggie dominate.

Just then, the Gardner family walked by our table. "Hi, Willie," Mrs. Gardner began, "and Maggie and Tom, so nice to see you." I hadn't heard Lobo called "Tom" in years. Mrs. Gardner paused, taking a second look at me. "Lornie, is that you? It's been years since I've seen you."

I barely knew this woman, unlike many families that frequented the Saturn Club. Listening to her pretentious voice intensified my negative feelings about going to the club.

"Yes, Mrs. Gardner, it's me." I was terse.

"Don't you live in Vermont or some wonderful place like that?" The voice was so insincere, just trying to make small talk, I felt. She was not going to give up on me.

"No, actually we left Vermont two years ago. We've been in Syracuse while my husband's been seeking his master's in social work. We're moving to Washington state soon."

I knew where this was going, but wasn't sure how to stop her. "Good Heavens!" she exclaimed. "What on earth is your Dad going to do with you moving so far away?"

"It'll be hard," I said, thinking of my own guilt. And it *would* be hard on Dad, I knew. He'd been dependent on Mom, and now he relied on Lobo and me. "But Lobo cooks for him a couple times a week and keeps an eye on him. I couldn't move that far away without knowing Lobo is right here." It's true, but I was sorry I was giving her all the scoop she desired. If I had thought it through, I would have had her direct the question to Dad; he was sitting right there. I started to tune her out as she made some other small talk. She smiled and went to be seated with her family.

As I looked around the room, recognizing the same old families, with new generations, I commented that some day I would write a book about these people. Lobo laughed and said that he had heard that from me before!

"I'm serious," I protested. I knew in my heart I had to process my life on paper and was quick to defend myself. "I may not write about these people, but I'm certainly going to write about the effect they and their lifestyle have had on our family." I didn't want to elaborate for fear of causing Dad's blood pressure to rise. But I wasn't going to let the pretentious standards of beauty and wealth corrupt my value system. And so the evening went, with Maggie and me carrying the weight of the conversation and Dad and Lobo quietly enjoying our company.

SIX

Dad

Relating with Dad on the emotional level I longed for was going to be difficult. I suspected that Dad's losses had become too much for him. It had been four years since we had buried Mom and sold Argyle Park. It was then, summer of 1990, when my relationship with Dad began changing. I realized I didn't know him any more. How long had he been this way? I wondered. Either Mom had been covering up for his inability to interact with the outside world, or her death was the last straw. He seemed hopelessly depressed. I knew that Mary's suicide had left its mark on both of them, but I had no idea that Dad had shut down so completely. I felt as though I had lost both parents.

I began to hate being around Dad. His hopeless demeanor and unwillingness to talk openly became a source of contention that I couldn't ignore. It was obvious that Dad wasn't willing to fend for himself. He had always been dependent on Mom. Lobo and I felt we needed to figure out a way for Dad to cope without Mom. A way for ourselves to cope without Mom. And a way for us to cope *with*

Dad. In the middle of the night I would roll over and stare at the ceiling wondering who would see Dad through. Lobo was already taking the initiative in helping Dad, just as he did for Mom. His adoption hadn't crippled him. Mom was his Mom, the Mom who saw him through his tough high school years, through Vietnam and through the years when he stopped communicating with us, the years Lobo needed to be away from Buffalo. And Dad was his Dad, the one who accepted him when he returned to Buffalo to help in Mom's final days.

But what about me? How could I not be there? How could I stop feeling guilty about leaving? How could I leave my father as his days were getting fewer? I wished Mom was still alive to help me deal with Dad. Without Mom, I needed to take a deeper look at myself, a deeper look at Dad. I needed to understand why Dad seemed so unapproachable.

Dad was almost eighty-three. He still had his faculties. He still had his physical health. He could, if he chose, still have control of his life. But he had lost so much. He had lost Mom. He had lost Mary. His home of forty-five years had been sold. His friends had been dying for years. As I struggled to understand why he had become so distant, I remembered how thoughtful he'd been to tell Nolie to cry her heart out when her father died. I started comparing that empathetic response to the death of Dad's sister. I realized the death of his beloved sister Elizabeth (when he was fifteen) was probably still buried deep in his heart.

Elizabeth was nine when she was struck with spinal meningitis. The closest source of medicine for the disease was Alaska. The medicine, which had to come by train, arrived too late. Elizabeth had died within three days of the onset.

Dad's brother Charles, my Uncle Chuck, was thirteen at the time of Elizabeth's death. From stories I've heard, my impression is that Dad and Uncle Chuck experienced typical sibling rivalry and that

Elizabeth had more of a special bond with Dad. In recollecting her death sixty-five years later, Dad told me she got sick on a Thursday and died that Sunday. Those days of the week were still ingrained in his head. I imagine he never got over losing her. He had lost his little sister; possibly his best friend.

Now, as I reflected on that special bond lost at such a young age, it helped me understand Dad's huge string of losses, his dear sister, both parents, one daughter and the light of his life, his wife. No wonder he couldn't handle looking at me. He couldn't bear anymore losses. And yet, I still wanted to feel connected with him.

∞

TAKING CARE of himself was something Dad never had to do. Dad was born to John Kimberly and Helen Virginia Walker in the summer of 1911. As the first-born son of well-off parents, he enjoyed many fine luxuries and privileges offered to few. Remembering Dad's upbringing helped me process his inability to cope with hardships.

Named after his uncle, Dad became William Henry Walker II. Dad struggled to find his place in this world. Even from birth, he missed a special bonding with his mother when she was unable to produce enough milk and hired a wet nurse to breast feed him.

But it wasn't only because of his wet nurse that he had a different relationship with his mother. Their relationship was foreign to me. Dad was chauffeured to school in a limousine. His meals were prepared by Mr. and Mrs. Cummings, the cooks. The house was cleaned by Margit who managed the entire home. They had a butler for a short while, Dad remembers. His name was James.

Dad's attachment to Buffalo and the social scene was deep-rooted. Helen and John belonged to the local society clubs, attended plays and concerts and, later in life, traveled abroad extensively. They balanced their lives by serving their community and church unselfishly.

John was a prominent businessman and churchman. At the turn of the century he was the president of his father's wholesale shoe business. During the depression he went into banking and became well known as an investment counselor. He was savvy with investments into his eighties. At the age of ninety, Granddaddy, as I knew him, would go downtown to his office every day. Mom told me he wrote letters and read, giving him needed space from Gran! After he died, a friend shared a story with me about those days in the late sixties when Granddaddy abhorred the busy traffic in downtown Buffalo. With his slow gait, he didn't have time to cross the street before the light changed. According to his friend, he would get half way across Main Street, shake his cane at the oncoming traffic and make sure they would let him cross at his own pace!

That seemed so out of character. Granddaddy was a quiet man and was often referred to as a saint by his family. Because of his modest nature, it was inconceivable that there were rooms, halls, and even a building named after him. I remember returning to Buffalo long after Granddaddy died and being introduced to a new priest at St. Paul's Cathedral, the church in which I was baptized and confirmed and where my ancestors went back for at least four generations. When the priest, a woman (it was 1990 and women were finally being ordained), heard my last name, she said, "Walker? As in 'room'?"

I looked puzzled, but quickly realized she was referring to The John K. Walker Room where most fellowship events at St. Paul's were held. It felt uncanny being recognized because of a room!

∞

HELEN, GRAN to all of us, was extraordinary. As a child, I was unaware of her privileged background and was in awe of her gregarious presence. Gran was a large woman, towering over Grandaddy, using her physical stature to its fullest.

Every Christmas Eve, Gran and Granddaddy would join our family for a formal dinner before the midnight church service. In our living room there was a certain chair designated for Gran. She would sit there with her old monogrammed denim bag at her side. Mary, Lobo and I would wait anxiously as she decided who would receive gifts first. She would call these her 'paper' gifts and tell us that the real presents would be given on Christmas Day. I never knew what was in the envelope she passed out to Mom and Dad, but they always "oohed" and "aahed" and thanked her and Grand-daddy profusely.

Gran would then look down into her bag with a devious smile telling us she knew she had something else, but couldn't see it.

"Oh, there it is," she would say, as she pulled out an envelope and gave each one of us a look of promise, adding, "I wonder who this one belongs to?" She played this game for years and had us hooked with great anticipation as to who would be next and whether or not the amount would increase!

On Christmas Day, our family, my aunt, uncle and cousins would all spend the afternoon at Gran and Grandaddy's. And more often than not, they invited those whom they called "the strays" from church and sometimes even the priest and his family. The formal dinner in the dining room was most memorable. Granddaddy, with his hearing aid turned off, would sit at the head of the table with a sweet smile on his face, oblivious to all the loud talk. Grandaddy may just have been the smartest of us all. One Christmas, Lobo put a tape recorder under the table and proved to us later how the noisy chatter of everyone talking at once was comical. Gran, sitting at the other end of the table, was ever present with her linen napkin fully unfolded on top of her large bosom. Under the table, there was a buzzer mounted into the floor under the dining room rug, something I never saw in anyone else's home. When Gran wanted Margit to bring something to the table, she would lean all her weight on her foot. With her foot on the buzzer, she let Margit know in no uncertain terms that she was ready to be served. That was Gran, the older woman.

I wish I had known Gran as a young woman. As a teenager at the turn of the century, she became known as a prominent tennis player. Her trophies are among my most prized possessions. One of them proclaims her the citywide champion for women's singles. But her athletic ability extended beyond tennis. Other trophies acknowledge her golf ability, and others proclaim her as a pool shark. The pool trophies baffled me, seeming so contradictory to the society in which I was raised. I always thought pool tables existed only in smoke-filled taverns. But in Gran's time, they were popular in the social clubs and in large recreation rooms in the grand old estates where she grew up.

Gran wasn't raised in Buffalo, but as a wealthy Philadelphian. Her father owned that city's prestigious DeWees department store. As a member of Philadelphia society, she was readily accepted into the ranks of the first families of Buffalo.

Her athletic trophies adorn my office space, bringing warm memories of the woman I remember as "the Sergeant." She had a presence about her that could be intimidating if you didn't know her well. As a Red Cross volunteer during World War II, she was Chairman of Staff Assistants, where her nickname "the Sergeant" was born.

I never really knew who "ran the show," as Mom would say, in that household. Whether it was Gran with her intimidating stature, or Granddaddy with his quiet but sharp ability to deal in the business world. They complimented each other and were respected highly by the community. They may have seemed well protected in their huge, old brick home with servants, situated in an exclusive part of the city, but the John K. Walker family couldn't shield themselves from the unexpected death of their nine year old daughter.

Elizabeth had been a glowing light in the lives of everyone with whom she came in contact. The Park School yearbook was dedicated in her memory. She was spoken of as an angel, fairy-like. And I believe debilitating to Dad, she was rarely, if ever, spoken of again. I can only imagine that he was told to keep his chin up and not cry.

∞

Dad was tall like his mother and distinguishably handsome. His attractive photograph hangs on the wall at St. Paul's Cathedral, Buffalo's historic downtown Episcopal Cathedral. Although he was the oldest child, Dad couldn't begin to follow in his parents' footsteps or those of Uncle Chuck. He was neither a businessman nor a sportsman. Chuck was his father's right-hand man, the son who accepted the bank partnership, the one who became an investment counselor with his father.

Dad tried hard to do what his parents wanted him to do. He went to the same college as his father, majoring in business, and he married the woman his parents wanted him to marry. But even that was a failure. Within six months they were divorced. His first wife, Dad confessed to me on the evening after Mom's memorial service, "preferred women!"

Mom told me about this marriage when she visited me in Seattle fifteen years prior to her death. But she never told me about the aspect of sexual preference. She just wanted to make sure that I heard about Dad's first wife straight from them before they died. Mom shared that the hardest part for her was that she and Dad weren't allowed to have a church wedding. The Episcopal Church didn't recognize second marriages at that time.

That didn't keep Mom or Dad from being involved in their

church. Dad with his active role at St. Paul's Cathedral, triumphed over Uncle Chuck. Today, it's Dad's photo, not his brother's, that is prominently displayed next to Granddaddy's in what once was the John K. Walker room and is now The Walker Room to include my dad, William Henry Walker II.

SEVEN

Questioning Everything

Buffalo, 1994

WITH THE dinner at The Saturn Club behind me, I looked forward to my night at the movies with Dad. As we got out of my car, Dad was smiling and seemed proud to be going out on a "date." A torrential rain was falling as we crossed the busy street to the theater. Dad's gait was slow, not unlike his father's, and on that dark, slippery road, it nearly gave me heart failure. But once inside the grand old theater, I relaxed.

The high ceilings with their sculpted moldings and gold trim brought an inviting sense of warmth and nostalgia. The movie was a special in a series of old films. *An Affair To Remember* with Cary Grant was the feature that night. The movie brought back fond memories. Sitting with Dad and watching the old-time love story on the big screen, I remembered how I had once looked up to him with unconditional admiration. How I used to think there was no one greater than he—the days he put me on his shoulders to watch a parade, when we would do yard work together, and when he would hold my hand walking down a street and explain how a gentleman always walked on the roadside to protect his woman.

Except for photos I've seen of Dad with me when I was an infant, I always remember him with gray hair. He was thirty-nine when I was born and had already started turning gray. Seldom did I see him without a pipe in his hand or embraced between his lips. His gray hair, bushy eyebrows and pipe always gave him an aura of dignity. Without a doubt he was a handsome man. Seeing Cary Grant reminded me of the handsome father I once adored. That night I thought maybe I could get close to Dad and tell him that the hardest thing about moving back out west was leaving him. But I didn't have the courage to risk my feelings. As though I were still a young child, I was fearful of feeling rejected. It broke my heart to think Dad might die without our expressing love for each other. I wondered if all adult children feel this way or if I felt these insecurities because I left Buffalo's protective circle after college. I tortured myself with "if onlys." Would Dad still have the ol' spark for me if only I hadn't deserted the enclave of Buffalo society, his only frame of reference. If only he hadn't lost Mom. If only Mary hadn't died. If only I stayed this time. I needed to know.

∞

College, Washington, DC, 1968

I HAD gotten out of Buffalo in 1968 when I headed to Washington, D.C. for college. What an incredible time to be in the District of Columbia. A lot of changes were going on in the world. If it wasn't Viet Nam protests or race riots, it was demonstrations for women's rights. For me, this was a whole new world.

The teaching career I had longed for had been put on hold. My

SAT scores were too low for a four-year program; instead, I opted for a two-year secretarial degree. The small women's college I chose was relatively conservative, but being in the heart of D.C. in 1968, Marjorie Webster Junior College offered a whole new perspective for a protected eighteen-year-old Republican from Buffalo, New York.

An announcement about community service was made at our freshman orientation meeting. Volunteering at Walter Reed Army Medical Center was one of the options. I jumped at the chance since I had loved being a Candy Striper at Buffalo's General Hospital the previous year.

The meeting with the volunteer coordinator was the same night I was to start my shift. She asked me if I had a preference of floors. "Anything but a locked psychiatric ward," I told her. "Wherever you need me most," I offered.

"Would you be willing to work on the amputee ward?" she pursued.

Imagining young guys curled up under the covers needing some TLC, I readily agreed. What I wasn't ready for was a room filled with men my age with exposed wounds. Some had lost one or both legs, an arm, or, as in Ralph's case, all four limbs. There had been no orientation, only a warning not to discuss politics or religion.

The coordinator took me up to the fifth floor where I was introduced to Ward 57, the amputee ward. Just outside the ward was a small room where I met the nurse in charge. With graying hair, the head nurse was short, stern and had a commanding presence. Without giving the coordinator a chance to introduce me, the nurse gave me orders. "Fill their water pitchers, listen to their stories, and if you're willing, give them massages," she told me tersely.

She shoved a plastic pitcher into my hand, led me to the tap water and said, "Fill this and follow me." I was in her command. No room for questions.

As she pushed open the double doors into Ward 57 and marched forward, I nervously followed behind. Partial limbs were set high on pillows or dangling from traction, some extremities with boils, others covered in bandages, but none with sheets. I felt all eyes upon us as I tried desperately to look at the men's faces, not their bodies. The nurse led me to a patient who was missing a leg, his partial limb in traction. His torso was tossing and turning as he called out angrily, "Nurse, where the hell are you?" seemingly in severe pain. I filled his glass, she handed him some pills. No sooner had he swallowed, than his eyes closed.

My commanding nurse turned around and led me back to a bed that was closest to the double doors next to the nurses' station. "This is Ralph," she said. "He's been here a few weeks." She paused slightly, "I bet he'd like some water." The nurse abruptly headed back to her little cubicle and to my relief never bothered with me again.

Ralph had lost one arm close to his shoulder, the other was intact just above the elbow. Both legs had been blown off slightly above the knee. In survival mode, I focused on his face. "My name is Lornie."

"Glad to meet you, Lornie," pointing and waving his bandage covered stump in my direction. My face must've been ashen. He spoke again. "This is your first time in an amputee ward, isn't it?"

I could hear myself take a deep breath and nodded my head. Usually nervous jabbering takes over when I don't know what to say, but I remained speechless.

"It's OK, Lornie. There's nothing to be afraid of." He waved his stump again. "You can shake it gently. It's healing well."

I cradled his shortened arm and looked back to his face. "Hardly anyone ever gets my name right on the first try." I decided I liked him right away and my nervous jabbering began. "Where were you stationed? My brother's in Nam now. He's on a barge in Cam Rhan Bay."

53

"Shhhhhh," Ralph said. "We're not suppose to talk about the war."

The one rule I had been given was already broken. "Oh God, I forgot, I'm sorry," I said and nervously filled his glass with water.

"Thanks, but you need to hold it up to my mouth, too," he said smirking a bit, but with a hint of annoyance in voice.

While I was tipping the glass toward Ralph so he could get a hold of the straw, he yelped out. "Oh God, my foot itches like crazy." I thought he was joking, but the irritated look on his face spoke volumes. "Oh hell, just get a nurse to turn me over and you can massage my back. Maybe that'll help."

The first squirt of sterile-scented hospital lotion on Ralph's back provoked another yelp. I learned quickly to warm up the lotion ahead of time. I had never massaged anyone's back before Ralph's dry, boney limbless body. My sister Mary used to pay me ten cents per foot to massage her precious feet. As I rubbed the lotion into Ralph's back, I thought of Mary's quirky requests. Not only did she want me to massage her feet, she wanted me to tickle them too. A light stroke up and down her foot would prompt a smile. "Again" she would tell me over and over. We always topped this little ritual off with expensive, flower-scented lotion that I would rub into her feet.

I looked down at Ralph wishing I could incite a smile by massaging his feet, relieving him of annoying itches. But that night, and the remaining Wednesday nights that fall and winter, it brought me joy to massage Ralph's back and give him some satisfaction of being touched.

Walking back to the dorm that first night I thought about how much I learned about limb loss. I was shocked to find out that amputees still have feeling sensations that seem like they come from their lost body parts. Phantom limb pain, they call it.

For me, working with Ralph became a spiritual experience and deepened my hatred for the war. Every Wednesday evening as I entered Walter Reed, knowing I had to be careful of what verbally transpired on Ward 57, I had to ask for God's grace. Ward 57 would stay with me forever. Along with some guilt-ridden Catholics from my dorm, I was still dutifully going to church that fall. But gradually I stopped. Repeating the creeds, singing the hymns and listening to outdated sermons, weren't helpful in understanding why people like Ralph had to endure such trauma. Why did the U.S. involvement in Viet Nam exist at all? I decided that God's grace was bigger than going to church.

In Buffalo, life issues seemed to be black and white for me, but in D.C. in 1968, I started questioning everything. Pot smoking was another barrier I crossed. It seemed as though I was one of the few young women in my dorm who had never smoked grass. One night toward the end of my first year, the dorm president was determined to get me stoned. I'll never forget that first "high."

She and some friends took me into the president's suite where we all crowded into her private bathroom and locked the door. It was in that tiny room that I toked and toked until they knew I would get high. I couldn't wipe the smile off my face and began acting giddy. Getting the munchies is the first thing I remember about being stoned. We all agreed to go out for beer and nachos. The Acropolis, our favorite local bar, was only a few blocks away. We gathered in the dorm lobby to sign out for the evening. I don't think our dorm mother had any idea what we were up to. All she witnessed was a group of silly girls going out for the evening. I loved listening to the bar music, which seemed more intense that evening, and watching my friends enjoying each other. Time became a blur as I joined in the frivolous chatter. That night I had a carefree feeling which I grew to love. Grass-smoking remained a part of my life on and off for many years. Not knowing Mary's susceptibility to drug abuse, I introduced her to marijuana. It was a summer evening in 1970 at our beach house in Canada. Mary found a joint in a pair of my blue jeans she had borrowed.

"This stuff is horrible for you," she scolded me. "If you don't get rid of it, I'm going to tell Mom and Dad."

I rebutted. "You have no right threatening me when you don't even know what it feels like."

Mary was twenty-one and already a mother. Maggie was a two-year-old. With her marriage falling apart, Mary had come home to live with Mom and Dad. I wanted her to see life my way and challenged her to smoke with me and check it out. I can't remember, but think it took little convincing. Her world was much different from mine. And yet, for once in our lives, she decided to go along with me.

Mom and Dad agreed to watch Maggie so Mary and I could take a walk. We headed down to the beach and smoked pot until I knew Mary was high. Similar to the first night I got stoned, our silly sides were acted out. We got down on all fours on the sandy beach and chased each other around some bushes. Mary lifted her leg as though she were a dog peeing. We laughed hard that night, but that was before drugs became a problem for Mary. She was hooked and I was the culprit.

That was my last summer in Buffalo, or as Mom would say, "so I thought." Graduation was behind me and a new career was waiting for me in D.C. But the secretarial life on Capitol Hill had lost its attraction. I had already worked there as an intern and was beginning to become disillusioned with politics. The job I landed was for retail lobbyists in the heart of downtown D.C. I was swept off my feet by my boss, the vice president of the company. I had a short-lived affair with him until I realized the affair became his weapon to take advantage of me. "Sexual harassment" wasn't a familiar term at that time. I was young and naive and fortunately found what I thought was a more prestigious job working in the infamous Watergate Building. That too came quickly to an end when I suspected corruption. I began questioning everything to do with the establishment. The power-hungry corporate world was not where I wanted to be, or belonged.

A girlfriend was working for a respectable insurance association in D.C. Her boss needed another secretary, so I applied and was accepted. I was making good money, but my longing for a truer meaning in life kept gnawing at me.

EIGHT

Pitcher of Beer

Washington, DC, 1972

M Y LIFE continued to change dramatically the summer of '72. It was a Friday night when my friends Val and Pam decided to go to College Park, Maryland. There was sure to be some action at the Varsity Grill, one of our favorite night spots near The University of Maryland. The three of us were sitting at a table sharing a pitcher of beer when we noticed a handsome young man sitting alone at a nearby table. We started joking about inviting him to our table when Pam made a serious dare. She offered a free pitcher of beer to either Val or me if we would invite this guy to join us.

I'm not one to let a pitcher of beer go wanting. I was out of my chair before Val had a chance. I paused for just a moment to absorb the coal dark hair, brown eyes, physically-fit and presumably tall physique of this strikingly wise-looking man. "Excuse me," got his attention. "My friends and I wanted to know if you'd like to join us."

He glanced up, with a look as though I was from Mars, but he surprised me with his politeness. "No thanks, I'm enjoying listening to the music." The D.J. was playing "Tommy" (by the Who) and the speakers were right over his head. I had been shot down by his desire to listen to that song.

"Ha! No pitcher for you."

Pam was off the hook. But I wasn't going to let her smugness stop me.

I kept an eye on him as he went up to the bar for another beer. Maybe if I got high I'd have the courage to try again. I persuaded Val and Pam to go outside to toke up with me. We left our coats on our chairs, not wanting any one to steal our table. But as I turned back to make sure our table was safe, I noticed two people had taken the table from the man whose name I didn't even know. Val and Pam were ahead of me, headed outside with my last joint. I couldn't resist as I passed the bar. "You've lost your table; you can still join us if you want."

"Sure."

I tried breaking the ice by putting out my hand, "I'm Lornie."

"Laurie?" he said as he shook my hand.

I repeated my name loudly over the din of the bar crowd and music. "No, Lornie....L-O-R-N-I-E." Spelling it always seemed to help.

"Rusty," he said without giving my name a second chance, and we walked single file through the crowd to our saved table.

As we sat down, I told him my friends had gone outside to smoke a joint and invited him to join us. Same as before, he'd rather listen to the music. I looked toward the door, debating about going outside, risking that Rusty would be gone when I returned. Val and Pam were coming back in. My joint was gone and I would have to rely on my own courage to converse with him.

"You owe me a pitcher." I told Pam as she pulled out her chair. She slapped me a five dollar bill with no argument. I waited for a break in the music to introduce Rusty to Val and Pam and headed to the bar to collect my well deserved pitcher. None of them looked up as I set the pitcher down and slipped into the last chair.

Story sharing came naturally with Rusty's easy going personality. No mind-altering courage was needed after all. I won more than a pitcher of beer that night. I won Rusty's heart. He came home with me that night and, except for a brief period, stayed by my side for over six years. He stayed with me through my hard-core anti-establishment days, my exodus from Mom, Dad and Buffalo, and the hardest part of my life, Mary's suicide.

∞

WHEN I met Rusty, he had just served two years in the army. That horrid draft had gotten him. The draft which I, along with so many of my peers, watched helplessly on TV one night in December of 1969. It was in the "rec" room of my college dorm where all of us young women waited anxiously for the fate of our boyfriends and brothers. Three hundred and sixty-six birth dates were randomly drawn one at a time, with the first 120 being the most likely to be drafted. For me, who had no boyfriend at that time, the only date I paid attention to was Lobo's. Sure enough, October 4th, Lobo's birthday, was drawn with that unlucky 120 batch. My brother would go to Nam. Rusty was luckier than most and was stationed in Germany. He had graduated in political science and knew all too well the political aspects of Viet Nam. The army further soured his outlook on politics, causing him to wonder what to make of his life. He had come home to be with his parents during this transition.

Together we attended peace rallies, ran from tear gas, and joined hundreds of thousands of young adults determined to change the establishment. But for Rusty, attending peace rallies wasn't enough. He became actively involved in McGovern's presidential campaign and tried to work within the system.

A few months into our relationship and after McGovern's failed election, Rusty's drinking increased and I began wondering whether our relationship would last. His clothes hung in my closet and his stereo had become part of my living room furniture. Rusty's depressed state brought a new silence between us. That silence was broken when he came home one night to announce he would be leaving for Iowa the next morning. We had been together only four months. He told me his Mom had helped him land a job with a newly elected congressman in her hometown of Des Moines. He packed his few belongings in one suitcase, told me I could keep the stereo and that he'd call in a week or so.

I knew I couldn't change his mind and decided my summer romance wasn't going to be the long-lasting relationship I had always dreamed about. I let Rusty slip out of my life just as easily as he had entered. Our good-bye was brief as I swallowed my tears and asked him to call as soon as he had an address. At night, I numbed my feelings with pot smoking and by day, kept busy with my secretarial job.

Five days later, early on a Saturday morning, I heard the doorbell, rolled out of bed, and peered through the peek hole; it was Rusty. After just one morning in the politician's office, his notion that politics was just a game was confirmed and he realized he couldn't handle that world. I never heard him say he couldn't live without me, but in his unassuming way, I knew he wanted to give our relationship more of a chance.

∞

SOME OF Rusty's college buddies had moved to Seattle, a place he longed to explore. Our evening talks revolved around Seattle as we began giving the west coast serious consideration. I had never been farther west than Colorado where I'd spent my vacation earlier that summer visiting Nolie. Nolie and I had remained in touch after leaving our sheltered lives on Argyle Park. She had moved to Denver for graduate school and introduced me to backpacking and the Rocky Mountains.

With Rusty, I began dreaming about driving across country and seeing all the beauty of the United States. I was eager to explore the country and introduce the beautiful Colorado Rockies to Rusty. My secretarial position was allowing me a comfortable life in D.C., but the job itself seemed too trivial. I was ready for a change and agreed to head west. A new, more earthy, less materialistic life could be in the making for me. I was psyched.

Unlike many of our peers, I couldn't just up and leave. To leave town with no job and little savings seemed irresponsible. Taking responsibility for myself was deeply ingrained; consequently, we stayed in D.C. for almost a year. I saved money while Rusty began his long road of acclimating to civilian life and reuniting with his friends and family.

It was the spring of '73 when our dream became a reality. I closed up my apartment, rented a U-HAUL, and returned to Buffalo with Rusty to say good-bye to Mom and Dad. Mom and Dad had gotten to know Rusty quite well that year. We had visited Buffalo a couple of times and I knew they liked him. I also knew that they were well aware that his presence in my life was leading me further to the left.

At breakfast that first morning in Buffalo, we began finalizing our cross-country plans. We needed to return our small U-HAUL that we had driven from D.C. and were considering renting a larger one to drive to Seattle. "How much is the U-HAUL going to cost?" Dad asked with his typical concern for money.

"I'm not sure. We're going to find out today," Rusty responded.

I looked at Dad. I knew he wasn't pleased with Rusty's laissez fair approach to life. As I suspected, his face tensed, his teeth gritting, I'm sure.

"One thing at a time," I jumped in. "We're returning the U-HAUL from D.C. this morning and we'll get the details then."

Mom scurried around the kitchen, dishing up cinnamon rolls, hoping, I imagine, the tension would ease once we started eating.

"Mary's hoping you'll drop by her apartment today," Mom said changing the subject.

I hadn't seen Mary or Maggie since I visited at Christmastime. Maggie had just turned five and, I was certain, was as sweet as ever. They had recently moved into a new place, which I heard was perfect. Mary rented the back half of a large three-story Victorian home.

It was settled. Rusty took care of the U-HAUL while I headed to Mary's.

Mary greeted me with a hug and one finger to her lips. "Maggie's napping." With a curling motion of her forefinger, Mary led the way, tiptoeing through her new digs. Each room was more charming than the previous. I just kept sighing "wow." The dining area had a huge bay window filled with plants. There were nooks and crannies everywhere. Even a tiny butler's pantry.

Maggie woke as we reached the third floor, her domain. Her mattress was on the floor in an alcove, surrounded with stuffed animals and one or two real kitties. Mary smiled as she lifted Maggie up and pointed toward me. "Look who's here!" I hadn't seen Mary this happy since Maggie was first born. I leaned over her shoulder and gave Maggie a kiss on the cheek. She rubbed her eyes, still waking up.

"You and your mom sure have the greatest new place," I said softly.

"And look out back," Mary chimed in as she put Maggie down. "Maggie and I are going to have a garden."

Mary's delight with her new life was refreshing. She was a loving and caring mom—full of creative ideas for Maggie and herself. Mary and her husband Dan had been separated a while and she was finally dating. I was genuinely happy for her.

When I returned to Argyle, Rusty was sitting at the kitchen table looking at the classifieds.

He looked up as the screen door slammed behind me. "I think it's too expensive to rent a U-haul. I'm thinking it might be cheaper to buy a truck."

Fortunately, Dad wasn't nearby to hear about this new idea. I didn't really care. Whatever we did, we knew we'd probably have to drive separately unless we found a vehicle that would haul my cute little Pinto. We spoke of many scenarios and finally ended up buying an old delivery truck.

∞

THE NIGHT before we journeyed across country, I remember sitting on Mom and Dad's four poster bed with the familiar white eyelet-laced cotton canopy overhead. I told Mom I needed to talk.

Mom stood by the foot of the bed, holding on to a post, looking me square in the eye, ready to listen.

"Moving out West means Rusty and I are going to live together." I had never told her that Rusty lived with me in D.C., although I suspect she knew.

"I assumed so," Mom said matter-of-factly. "But that doesn't mean I condone it. Times have changed and I trust you know what you're doing."

I didn't know then how difficult it is to be a parent and learn when to trust your child's judgment. But I did know that Mom knew what it was like to leave home.

With tears in my eyes, I affirmed my thoughts aloud. "Thanks for understanding." I stood up and gave her a big hug, feeling fortunate that she seemed to recognize my need to leave. That didn't minimize the pain on her face as she watched from the sun porch, or the tears streaming down mine, as Rusty and I backed out of 19 Argyle Park that next morning in May.

NINE

Mom

IT WAS easy to see why Mom could understand that I needed to establish my own roots. She left her own mid-western roots for Buffalo in her late twenties. My husband Tom has reminded me more than once that Mom's strength and great sense of humor came out of hardship.

She was the youngest of four Minnesota farm children, raised by a single mother. She barely got to know her father. In 1915, when Mom was five, her father went to the Mayo Clinic in Rochester, Minnesota with cancer and never returned. Mom had one fond memory of her father—he played "nosy-nosy" with her. Every so often, even as an adult, Mom would share her nose kiss with me—her way of keeping her father alive. And now, I continue his legacy when I rub noses with my own children, telling them that's the one memory Mom had of her father.

The only photo I have of him was taken in the courtyard of the Mayo Clinic. Dying of cancer, in a hospital almost 200 miles from his family, the photo spoke of his pride. Sitting in a straight back chair reading a newspaper, he posed for his family, wearing a sweater vest with sports jacket. In this black and white photo, a tie tucked into his sweater and pen clipped in the pocket of his sports jacket, he had a remarkably distinguished look. With a well-trimmed mustache, Thomas Prideaux was a handsome man, barely graying, at the young age of fifty, when he died.

He had been a townsman (today's councilman) and ran the country store and feed shop in Rushmore, Minnesota. Rushmore, still only a small town in the 1990s, was a blink in the road in the 1890s when Thomas met Bessie Stewart. Mom's parents, Bessie and Thomas, were married when Bessie was twenty-seven and a promising young school teacher. Back then, if you were a female teacher and wanted to get married, you were forced to resign. Bessie gave up teaching for Thomas. They had two boys and two girls. Only thirty-nine when Thomas died, Bessie had to raise the children herself. With determination and high expectations of their children, Bessie went back to school and became re-certified to teach.

Bessie had her oldest daughter, Edith, look after her younger sister, Lorna (my mother). Mom made it hard for her big sister Edith. She always told us she was "the class clown" and Edith would often have to bail her out of trouble. She misbehaved fairly often and would be sent to the principal's office. She told me she wanted to prove to the other kids that although her mother was a teacher in that school, she wasn't shown favoritism.

Mom never shared much about her childhood. And by the time I started searching for family history, Mom was entering the final stages of her brain disease and was unable to communicate. But I heard some of their early history from my aunt Edith when, due to her poor eyesight and inability to write letters, she made me a tape recording shortly before her death.

The Prideaux family limped through the depression and never had much, material-wise. Edith told me that it never bothered them when they were young because they didn't know better. But later on they knew. It became important to Mom to climb the social ladder and make herself known in the world, similar to how she made herself known in grade school.

When Edith went off to college, Mom was in high school and had to be left to her own devices. Mom was a survivor and knew what she had to do. She pulled her act together, graduated from high school and went on to get her secretarial degree.

After a couple of starting secretarial positions, Mom's life turned around when she became the executive secretary for the minister of the distinguished Gethsemane Episcopal Church, in Minneapolis. Edith was well connected with church ministry and pulled strings to help Mom get an interview. That's all it took. Mom could sell herself. Her gregarious personality, sense of humor, quick wit, and ability to establish rapport easily won over the heart of the Reverend Austin Pardue. Mom was raised a Presbyterian, but the Reverend Pardue became her mentor and she was soon swayed by the Episcopal church.

A few years into the job, her heart was broken when the Reverend Pardue accepted the position of Dean of St. Paul's Cathedral in Buffalo, New York. He was the father she never had, the role model of what a family man could be. But her mourning was soon shortened when she received a phone call which she told me about numerous times. I can hear the tapes as though it were yesterday: "Lorna, it's Austin Pardue. I love my new job here in Buffalo, but I need help. Would you be willing to move?"

In every retelling of this story, Mom told me she didn't think twice. "Absolutely," I can hear her say. She wasted no time in packing her belongings and headed to Western New York as soon as she could. She became Austin Pardue's assistant, as the Parish Visitor and Youth Director of St. Paul's Cathedral, Buffalo, opening the door to Willie's life. Willie is what she always called Dad, except for the times when he didn't appear to be listening, then he became William Henry.

Before Willie, Mom had several other beaus as she moved up in the world in her life as a secretary. She once told me about a young man she was engaged to. One sunny summer afternoon they were at a picnic together and went out for a boat ride. She had a reputation as a party girl and loved to take things to extremes. She told him she didn't want to marry him and threw the engagement ring overboard! I imagine Mom had been drinking and was feeling her oats.

It was in Buffalo where Mom started a new life for herself. Dreams that were unspoken, dreams she never thought possible, were now within reach. She understood why some people need to go further than their surroundings, unlike Dad who had trouble understanding anything beyond the only world he knew. He was born and raised in Buffalo and, except for some traveling he did with Mom, he had little interest beyond his familiar surroundings, no dreams of his own.

TEN

Unrealistic Expectations

Seattle, 1973

Rusty and I headed to Seattle with a blank slate. Neither of us knew what we wanted to do with our lives. But we did know we didn't want to be part of the "establishment." The lure of the unknown in our westward adventure became the underlying hope we desperately wanted.

Until Colorado, the journey across country was uneventful, staying in cheap motels and an overnight with a n'er-do-well buddy of Rusty's. My bright orange 1972 Pinto led the way with Rusty following in "George," an old spaghetti delivery truck painted brown. Looking much like a UPS truck, George was filled with every last belonging. We spent a few nights with Nolie in Denver and took day hikes in some of the most scenic countryside I had ever seen. For me, Colorado became the gateway to the west, the gateway to my new life.

From Colorado, we headed north into Wyoming and Montana, camping the rest of the way. Our orange and brown caravan was quite the sight as we pulled into a riverside campground in eastern

Montana. George was twice as tall and twice as long as my little Pinto. Nearby campers gawked as Rusty opened the back doors of George to retrieve our camping gear. He pulled out his tall speaker set, an old rocking chair and an upholstered foot stool. They must have thought we were squatters setting up home!

We were novice campers with heavy old flannel-lined sleeping bags, a couple of funky canvas tarps (no tents) and looked very citified. With no cooking gear, or cooler, we fudged for dinner. Leaving George filled with our precious possessions, we drove off in the Pinto in search of food. Returning shortly, I pulled out a six pack of beer and placed it on the picnic table. But I imagine it was the McDonald's bag and French fries that put us over the edge in the minds of the other campers. We seemed to have had no taste.

The second night brought rain. We pulled into a new campground and prepared for a night inside the truck. Rusty crawled into the back of George and rearranged as much furniture and boxes as possible. There we formed a tight space in which to curl up in our sleeping bags and sleep away the rain.

The sun was glistening on the damp grass when I dragged myself out of George the next morning. This was the day we were going to reach Seattle. I was psyched. Without hesitation, Rusty and I followed each other in search of a McDonald's. Using the drive-up window, I pulled ahead of Rusty and ordered my usual Egg McMuffin and coffee. George, with Rusty behind the wheel, loomed in my rear view mirror. Rusty ordered an Egg McMuffin with his morning ritual, a Pepsi. In tandem, we pulled away ready for our last haul.

After trucking across the yellow and brown dry terrain of Eastern Washington, the dramatic features of the Cascade Mountain Range seemed surreal. Curve after curve, we promised each other we'd return to these areas and explore the depths of the mountains. George didn't like the Cascades. In my rear view mirror I could barely see Rusty as he and George dropped farther behind. I slowed almost to a complete stop until Rusty was able to pull beside me. With our windows down, he yelled, "Keep going." I pulled ahead and held my breath as I watched him struggling, as George puttered behind me. By some miracle, George and Rusty made it to the summit where we stopped for a break and prayed George would make it the rest of the way.

George did make it to Seattle, but died on a busy street in front of a tiny shopping center near the University of Washington. Rusty's college friend Rick was expecting our arrival in Seattle that evening, but we couldn't locate his address on our map. Oh, to have a cell phone in 1973! It was still light when Rusty headed to the shopping center to call Rick, leaving me standing guard.

My feeling of aloneness was overwhelming as I watched Rusty cross the unfamiliar busy street into an unknown shopping center in this seemingly large uncharted city. "Take a deep breath, Lornie," I told myself. More than anything, I was worried about traffic as there was no shoulder and we were blocking the right lane. The twenty minutes Rusty was gone seemed like an hour. He returned with great news—we were within minutes of Rick's place and a tow truck was on its way.

The first few days were spent taking care of George, touring Seattle, and best of all, going hiking. Rick took us to Goat Lake near Mt. Rainier where that majestic mountain loomed above us. I was hooked. Seattle and its surroundings had captured my heart.

We found our own apartment within a week of arriving. I couldn't stand one more night in Rick's apartment, hanging out with his grad school friends from the University of Washington. Their philosophical, in-depth discussions tapped into my insecurities surrounding my lack of a four-year college education.

Rusty and I moved into the upstairs of a large, old, Victorian home on Capitol Hill. From the bay window in our living room we had a peek view of Mt. Rainier. I knew I was where I was supposed to be. Our lives fell into place as though everything had been carefully planned. Our landlord painted houses for a living and offered Rusty full-time work. I was able to draw unemployment from my secretarial job in D.C. and had no regrets taking advantage of "the system." I felt animosity toward the way our government was run; it was with leisure that I searched for what would satisfy me most.

That fall, Sam and Bonnie, two more of Rusty's college friends, moved to Seattle. "Iowa transplants," we called them. Our flat was spacious with a large second bedroom where Sam and Bonnie stayed for a few months. With no children, the four of us were carefree young twenty-somethings. I spent most of that winter exploring Seattle, making friends and enjoying my new found freedom.

I was feeling upbeat, learning to live my life on my own terms. The secretarial world seemed like another lifetime. Buffalo and Washington, D.C., had become part of my past. For almost a year, I rarely thought about Buffalo, until Mary's life began falling apart.

∞

Spring 1974

THE RING startled me. Rusty and I had already gone to bed. The phone never rang in the middle of the night. I fumbled for the light to find the receiver.

"Lornie?" I heard Mom's voice.

Mom wouldn't be calling that late unless it was serious. I thought something must have happened to Dad and listened for more.

"Mary's in the hospital, but she's going to be all right."

"A car wreck?" I can still hear myself saying.

"No. She slit her ankles. You know, like when someone slits their wrist."

By this time I was sitting on the edge of my bed in disbelief. This kind of thing happened to other people, not our family, I thought. Stuttering, I searched for words, "But, but she's OK, right?"

Mom assured me that she was going to be all right and said she would call back the next day when they knew more.

I was still trying to comprehend everything, but agreed it would be best to talk again in the morning. As always, I ended our conversation with, "I love you."

"We love you, too." And Mom was gone.

I've always had trouble figuring out the time difference between coasts, but lying in bed that night, I calculated that it must have been the middle of the night for Mom. How could she possibly sleep? Her daughter wanted to kill herself. I couldn't sleep either, finding it hard to believe that Mary was desperate enough to consider taking her own life. She had been severely depressed before, but I never knew she would want to kill herself. Mary was twenty-five then and had been living with Mom and Dad on Argyle. I never did hear why she vacated the wonderful old duplex I had visited the previous summer. But I did know that Maggie was being shuffled back and forth between Mary and Dan. She was only six and obviously going through experiences no six-year-old should have to deal with. I was relieved to learn Maggie was at Dan's that evening.

As Mom promised, she called the next day with details. It was in the bedroom we shared as little girls on Argyle Park that Mary had tried to end her life. The crayon marks we made on the wall above our beds were long gone. Fancy contemporary pink and white striped wallpaper replaced the old familiar rose petal paper I remember as a child. But the beds were the same. It was in one of those twin beds that Mary took a knife to her ankles, cutting the arteries that linked her to life.

"Dinner's ready," Mom had called up the stairs to Mary. No response. Margit, my grandmother's maid, was polishing silver, helping Mom get ready for Easter.

"I'll go get her," Margit offered. Margit knew Mary well. She had helped Mom during the early adoption days, during Mary's teenage depression, during her bout with mononucleosis and, most recently, through Mary's divorce. She was Mom's confidante and adored Mary.

Margit opened Mary's bedroom door to silence. Mary was lying unconscious in a pool of blood.

The frantic sound of Margit's voice, the sirens blaring as the ambulance pulled onto Argyle Park, and the blood-soaked mattress are images, I imagine, Mom and Dad could never forget. Mary survived with seemingly only minor physical damage. But what we didn't know was that her downward spiral was in full force.

As I began learning from Mom more about Mary's preceding year in Buffalo, I discovered it wasn't her first attempt to threaten her own life, sending out silent screams for help. An earlier attempt, swallowing toilet bowl cleaner, made her terribly nauseous, but word of that incident had never left the confines of 19 Argyle.

∽

I DECIDED to be with Mom and Dad for Easter and flew home the next weekend. Mary had been released from the "regular" hospital and committed to Buffalo State Hospital. The grounds of Buffalo's mental hospital were extraordinary. The landscape, designed by Frederick Law Olmstead, once covered more than 200 acres of trees and rolling meadows. As described by Lauren Belfer in her book *City of Light* (published by Bantam Dell in 1999), in 1901 the patients "grew their own vegetables, milked their own cows, raised their own pigs. They possessed a bubbling brook to stroll along. A

75

baseball diamond. A music conservatory. A greenhouse......a paradise at the edge of the city."

I visited Mary twice that weekend. The grounds, still covered with lush gardens, shrubs and grassy alcoves, offered a classy, estate-like feeling as I walked through the lofty iron gates. Entering the huge, old ivy-covered brick building which I had driven by for many years, I felt "The Twilight Zone" come alive. Unfamiliar with the psychiatric world, I walked through the corridors with an uneasy feeling. I had never imagined that the people behind those walls—the place we used to call "The Nut House"—were real. There were people with some of the weirdest behaviors I had ever seen. One tall guy with a Frankenstein presence followed Mary and me to the front porch where we were to visit. She told me not to pay attention to him, that everyone there was crazy, including herself. I never considered her crazy.

Our visit was short. Mary wasn't about to open up to me. I found myself making small talk. I didn't know what else to do as I looked out from the porch with its short brick wall and open air surrounded by heavy metal bars. Looking out onto the road where, only a few blocks from Argyle Park, we drove by often as kids, pinching our noses, holding our breath and treating that institution as if it were poison. Mary had become part of that poison.

Why did we treat Buffalo State Hospital as poison? Who exactly were the patients there? Were they people who couldn't cope, people who behaved 'abnormally,' people who couldn't fit into society's norms? Mary, once contender for the Queen of Buffalo's debutante ball, was now probably considered an outcast from the social world I had fled. The world which made me feel inferior and insecure. I had long since given up trying to fit in, trying to live up to the pretentious image that pulled at all my personal values. My answer had been to flee.

But it was different for Mary. She had played their game and had become so enmeshed in Buffalo's social world, she probably saw no way out. Mary was well read and seemed to have an in-depth understanding of the world. She believed in feminism. The Towne and Country *staff who photographed her in 1971 wrote a wonderful description . "She is her own strong-willed kind of woman. Despising dishonesty and war. Discouraged by provincial attitudes of people reluctant to experience and explore." I can only imagine she felt trapped.*

The next day I went again. After the Easter church service, Mom, Dad and I marched into Mary's tiny private bedroom. We probably talked about the Easter service. Mary kept her head down, not saying a word. She probably answered our tedious, safe questions, but, for me, the visit was excruciating. I'd be flying back to Seattle that night and didn't want to leave with such a horrible image. Mom and Dad said good-bye and headed for the car. I told them I'd be there in a minute.

I turned around and looked at Mary and said, "Can't you even smile? I made a special trip to see you."

How stupid of me. She looked at me with angry eyes and blatantly said, "No."

"I'm sorry." I left on that dismal note, with no other response from Mary.

I could have kicked myself as I walked out to the car. I knew it was a ridiculous statement, an unrealistic expectation, but I couldn't bear the silence between us or the sadness of her existence.

How many other times in my life had I said stupid things to Mary, always trying to make things right between us. The comparisons we made with each other ran too deep.

ELEVEN

Magnolia Bluffs

Seattle, 1974

MARY MOVED back in with Mom and Dad after her release from Buffalo State Hospital. I didn't keep in touch with her then. I had allowed the 3,000 mile distance to become the needed barrier to separate myself from the life I wanted to leave behind.

ACCUMULATING HOUSE plants became my new passion. Our southern facing living room provided us with unending natural light. Amazed at how readily things grew in the Northwest, Bonnie and I started acquiring house plants by the dozen. We learned how to start roots from cuttings and turned our front porch into a major transplanting area. By February, we were outdoors turning the soil for a mini-vegetable garden. It was in May, not long after returning from Buffalo and seeing Mary, that we came up with the wildest idea.

I can visualize Sam, Bonnie, Rusty and I sitting at our kitchen table admiring our plants. Rusty passed the joint to me. After taking a long drag, I passed it to Sam. We continued passing the joint around our old vinyl-topped thrift store table.

"Maybe we could make some money off of all these plants," Rusty fantasized.

"And just what do you have in mind?" I can hear myself asking.

"I don't know," he answered, looking at Bonnie and me. "You're the growers."

"I could get into it," I said, "but I have no clue how to begin." In my stoned state, I began taking the idea seriously.

"I could help get us started," Sam chimed in. "I've gotta get something out of my business degree."

"Lornie would have to deal with the customers." Bonnie said. Bonnie's not as much of a people person as I am and was probably the most apprehensive.

"With my unemployment running out, I really do need to figure something out," I continued.

It was in those stoned moments that I became convinced I could be an entrepreneur. The four of us set out to create The Mother Earth Plant Shop. Even Mom had her hand in it, giving us the idea for the name when she told me about a new plant shop in Buffalo called Mother Earth. The 3,000 mile distance allowed me to breathe and grow on my own, but somehow Buffalo and Mom still managed to play a role in my life.

We found a small affordable storefront for rent on Queen Anne Hill. Peeking through the windows, we could see the remains of an old beauty salon. The shop was at a bus stop on Boston Street, five short blocks off of Queen Anne Avenue. It was perfect. After jotting down the rental phone number on scrap paper, we called the landlord from the closest phone booth. All on the same day, we met the owner at the shop, signed a lease, made a deposit, and the deal was done. We had a minimal amount of money to invest and needed to make use of our rented storefront quickly. We spent a few frantic weeks fixing it up and were ready for business within a month. The provocative beauty poses were torn off the wall with vigor. Bonnie and I were women of the seventies and not about to allow sexy bodies be part of our decor.

We ripped out the old floor, finding layer upon layer of cracked, warped linoleum. Like layers of lost life, I scraped down to the bone, peeling off old messages, old assumptions, attempting to find my own earthiness and begin replanting my life. We built hanging shelves, plastered walls, and painted everything until the new earthy image had taken hold. We hauled an old claw foot tub from the back alley and filled it with plants. Mother Earth's reality surrounded us.

Sam organized our bookkeeping and Rusty created an extraordinary three-dimensional flower pot sign. Sawn from a large sheet of plywood, and painted bright blue, green, yellow and orange, the huge "Mother Earth Plant Shop" sign hung over the front door and could be seen easily from the east as we crested Queen Anne Hill and from the west as we headed toward Lake Union. We were young, and like the sign, vibrant and seemingly indestructible.

∞

I can't remember whose idea it was to have Mary come to Seattle. I could have made the offer, Mary could have initiated it, or, what is my strongest guess, Mom thought it would be best. I do know that it was at this time that I started consciously carrying the burden of Mary's troubles.

Rusty and I agreed that Seattle would be a good place for Mary to visit. We were settling into our new lives. We had been there a year, established new friendships, and could offer her a secure place to stay. Mary was a gifted artist. She had designed needlepoint for a local craft store, but for me, her most talented work was evident in her watercolors. I was hopeful she could find artistic inspiration in a new environment. Buffalo seemed to pull at her dark side—the mystery of her birth parents haunting her, the recent divorce, the Walker money intensifying her anger. Could it be that in Seattle, known as the gloomiest, grayest city in the United States, Mary could find light? At least she was coming in the summer; I wouldn't want her to experience a Seattle winter. But I was naive to think that all Mary needed was a change of scenery.

Maggie had permanently moved in with Dan when Mary was in the State Hospital. Once Mary was released, she returned to Argyle to live with Mom and Dad and saw Maggie less often. Before Mary headed to Seattle, Mom had warned me that the scene on Argyle had gotten ugly. One night at dinner, Mary had let her anger at Dad get out of control when she flipped over the long heavy dining room table toward him. He was barely bruised physically that night, but their relationship became scarred for life. I never knew what triggered Mary's anger over dinner, but she always took it out on Dad, especially since he had inherited a substantial amount of money from Gran and Grandaddy. It seemed Mary felt they didn't share enough of their new wealth with us kids.

Mary came to Seattle that summer of '74; that summer I spent endless hours getting the plant shop on its feet and Rusty painted houses from dawn 'til dusk. We gave Mary the expected visitor tour, the places we had grown to love. We took her to Pike Place Market, the downtown farmer's market rich with life—the Hmong men and women selling cut flowers; the smelly fish stalls where the fish sellers compete flinging purchased fish to customers; the crafts people; and the street musicians serenading passers-by for a buck. Mt. Rainier, the volcanic mountain towering above the cascade mountain range with its awesome spiritual presence, and the newly opened Discovery Park with its long trails and beach walks, were also on our "tourist list." We took Mary to all these places in hopes of brightening her spirits. Even in her subdued state of mind, in which she made little effort to connect with us, Mary fell in love with the area and decided to stay.

Sam and Bonnie had found a place of their own, leaving us with the spare bedroom for Mary. Her room was more than ample. Facing south, it was bright and spacious with a long window bench filled with plants.

Six days a week Bonnie and I shared long hours running the plant shop. Business was off to a slow start, but we agreed to give it at least six months. We placed ads in *The Queen Ann News* and had radio spots on Seattle's popular station 92.0 KZAM.

∞

THAT FALL our rent on Capital Hill increased, and we decided to move to more affordable housing. Mary moved with us. She helped out with food stamps and gave us a small amount of her allowance from Dad. But she rarely chipped in with household chores and spent most of her days getting stoned in her bedroom, learning how to read tarot cards.

Mary's lack of motivation to take responsibility grew old. We encouraged her to get a job and possibly her own place. Instead, her defenses took over and she decided to head to San Francisco to visit Lobo. Rusty and I were eager to have a break and helped her make a bus trip to San Francisco happen.

It was late fall, probably November, when Mary and I entered the bus depot world.

There was trash everywhere, filthy bathrooms reeking of urine, and a class of people with whom I was unfamiliar. Homeless people were curled up against the wall using their coats for pillows, beggars had their hands open or hats on the floor in front of them, and distant announcements were made over a loud speaker.

The bus to San Francisco was delayed two hours and I had no desire to hang around. Mary agreed that it was senseless for me to wait with her. Feeling spared, I headed home.

Several hours later, as Rusty and I were settling in to a quiet evening at home, the phone rang. It was Melanie, a Seattle friend Mary had met through us.

"Mary's here and she's not in good shape."

"What the hell? I left her at the bus station."

"No. She's here with me. She won't talk and she's on the floor in my laundry room curled up in the fetal position. Lornie, she's totally shut down. I think we should call an ambulance. You need to get over here."

"What happened?" I was totally confused.

"I think she's having a weird drug reaction."

I wasn't sure what to do. Melanie is a take-charge person, so I told her to call the ambulance if she thought that was the thing to do, and I'd be there as soon as possible.

Melanie lived below the Magnolia bluffs, just south of Discovery Park. Her beachfront cottage was one of three homes, accessible only by foot. Rusty parked the car in a small parking area above the beach. The trail head was unlit, but from our frequent visits to Melanie's, we were able to instinctively find the familiar trail. The tide was high, forcing us to use Melanie's rickety planks to her porch.

"The ambulance is on the way," Melanie told us and led me down the hall to where Mary was curled up with her head between her knees and chest.

"Mary?" I said. She didn't respond or look up.

"She's conscious, but I can't get any more out of her. First thing I knew I heard someone calling from the blackberries behind my house," Melanie backtracked. "Mary was stumbling out of the bushes saying she hurt her leg. She told me she was trying to climb down the ridge side to my house."

The medics came within minutes of my arrival. Melanie and I shared what we knew, including the drug possibility. They had seen other cases like this and decided she should go to the emergency room and possibly be committed to psychiatric care.

Transferring Mary from Melanie's waterfront home below the steep, muddy bluffs of Magnolia to the ambulance was an ordeal in itself. The tide had receded enough for them to carry her on a stretcher along the beach, then work their way up the bluff on an unlit, narrow, slippery path behind the next home. I followed Mary and the crew along the path, barely putting one foot in front of the other.

My first and only ambulance ride was in the quiet vehicle that night. No sirens. Just the spooky image of Mary lying on her back with her eyes staring into nothing.

I tried talking to her. "I don't know what to do. I probably should call Mom and Dad."

She just lay there, stared at me, then turned away. She was committed that night in her comatose-like state.

After that night, Rusty and I agreed Mary could no longer live with us. She was released after 24 hours and, with the help of social workers, found a tiny basement apartment on Seattle's Capitol Hill.

∞

THE MORNING Mary was released, I spoke with Melanie.

"Mary shared one thing with me a few days ago," Melanie said. "She told me she got a phone call from some photographer in New York who had seen her pictures in *Town and Country*. He wanted to photograph her. She hung up on him."

"The beauty issue," I said. "I think Mary's had more than enough of Buffalo society and the beauty image she's had to live up to. It's hard for me to relate." I had never had that problem.

I could never stand next to Mary without feeling compared. From the day I was born, there are family photographs that tell the story, photos of Mary jumping into the picture when mine was being taken, photos few and far between of Mary and me willingly standing or sitting next to each other.

Mary must have been ten or eleven, and I a year younger, when one afternoon, we were waiting for the buses to pull in to school to take us home. It was our first year at Park. I was in third grade, Mary was in fifth. It was our first day to go home at the same time. Mary and I had been standing side by side talking when she stepped away for a moment.

A boy came up to me. "Is that your sister?" he asked.

"Yeah," I replied not thinking much about it.

"She can't be, she's so pretty." He didn't say anymore; he didn't have to. It was what was left unsaid that stuck with me.

I responded with what seemed an easy explanation. "She's adopted and I'm not." To me, she was the lucky one.

The irony of how Mary and I envied each other still amazes me, my admiration for her beauty, physical coordination and intelligence and her longing for legitimacy and a sense of belonging; my feeling inferior because I didn't live up to society's expectations of having good looks and a high I.Q. and her searching for inner peace, innate from the mother who gave her birth. Neither of us accepted ourselves for who we were.

At the time, I failed to understand the reasons for Mary's attempts on her life and the pain she carried. It wasn't until much later when Mom and Dad told me she was manic depressive. I still don't know whether that was a fact, or whether Mom and Dad speculated it. I knew she had many issues with her adoption and had distress over her divorce, but her struggles were foreign to me. I always had my own struggles and insecurities and constantly compared myself to her. With little effort, her report cards shined with "As." No matter how hard I tried, "Cs" dominated my report cards.

My brain never seemed to function as well as Mary's. I had wanted to become an elementary teacher, but due to low SAT scores, my college advisor said I would never make it in a four-year program. Listening to the advisor, instead of pursuing my dream, I chose a secretarial program. I had little faith in my educational pursuits and felt I had no choice.

At the two-year college, after a general entrance exam, I was pulled aside the first week for special testing. I can hear the examiner now. "You're dyslexic; too bad they hadn't figured that out when you were in second grade, because now it's too late." I never felt more doomed—there I was a young adult preparing to enter the world on my own, and I was told "It's too late."

I have no memory of being encouraged by Mom and Dad. Instead, I remember put-downs made teasingly by Mom and her half-hearted compliments, which were always nullified because she would tell me she "didn't want my head to swell." It was the fifties and parents assumed "the American Dream" just happened. Except for Dr. Spock, no books or special parenting classes were offered as they are today.

It wouldn't be until five years after Mary died that I finally pursued my dream. At thirty-two, I had been a teacher's aide for over seven years. The teachers I worked with encouraged and convinced me to seek my teaching degree. Certain of failure, I went to be tested by the Washington State Association for Adults with Learning Disabilities. New sophisticated tests proved my suspicions that I had a learning problem involving auditory processing. I couldn't listen to others or read for any length of time without getting things jumbled in my head. For another $500 there were other tests that would provide more in-depth information. I chose not to sink more money into the system, but to use common sense, concentrating on visual and tactile ways of learning. I taught as an aide during the day and took prerequisites toward my teaching degree at night. I recorded lectures, transcribed them, and made flash cards. My friend Cathy quizzed me over and over. It was persistence that pulled me through five years later. After marriage, one child, and at seven months pregnant with number two, I graduated Magna Cum Laude in Special Education and Psychology. I persevered and moved beyond my learning difficulties. I made it. I went the distance.

There's a song I love to listen to by Libby Roderick which pulls me out of the darkness when my spirits are low. My favorite line is, "It takes a whole lot of looks to be a Homecoming Queen, but living takes a whole lot more."

TWELVE

Respite

Buffalo, 1994

D AD WAS staring at the television and seemed oblivious to my tangential thoughts. For all I knew, he, too, may have drifted off to old parts of his life when he sat and stared at the TV. Thinking about my upcoming evening with Maggie and seeing all the TV coverage about every aspect of Jackie Kennedy Onassis' life, it was no wonder I had become lost in the world I had so deeply buried.

I took a deep breath, realizing I needed to think about my day. I made a sandwich for Dad, reminding him I would be heading out shortly to meet my friend Karla for lunch.

As I drove to the restaurant, I gave thanks for Tom's wisdom in helping me break up my emotion-fraught week by having lunch with my good friend. I couldn't wait to see Karla that afternoon. She understood me.

Karla was standing in front of Just Pasta, the restaurant that had become our favorite meeting place. With open arms and her playful giggle, Karla welcomed me with a huge hug. We both gushed over each other's appearances as the waitress led us out to the patio.

We had barely sat down when Karla threw out questions about my life much faster than I could answer. I ignored them.

"I've been totally wrapped up in the news about Jackie's death," I said. "She always reminded me so much of Mary. I can't think about anything else."

"Tell me. Tell me everything." Karla's enthusiasm always warmed my heart.

"I keep playing old tapes over and over. The one I can't get out of my head is Mary's Roanoke Street Bridge jump."

"I remember your telling me about her setting herself on fire." Karla's tone became somber.

"Hearing it on the radio was so unnerving." I started rambling.

∞

Seattle—1975

I VISITED Mary on and off during the two months she was in Harborview. We never spoke much. I would tell her about my day. She would listen and show me her scars from the skin grafting.

Mary experienced a great deal of physical pain during that time but rarely spoke of her emotions. She did confess to me that she got "high" in order to get the courage to set herself on fire that horrid day of the jump. And yet I felt, even without the drugs, there must have been silent screams within her to be saved when she chose such an open, public setting in an attempt to end her life.

I made my own assumptions about her state of mind. Prior to the jump, Mary hadn't worn a dress in a long time. She wore sweaters and baggy pants, in an effort I imagine, to cover up her beauty and reach out for a deeper internal love. Now there was little beauty to cover up. I had hoped that maybe, since she miraculously survived and was still able to walk, she could see it as a sign for another chance in life, a chance, I felt, to find the self-worth she so desperately longed for.

With Mary's unwillingness to talk much, I found our visits difficult. I had my own life to deal with then and felt my world couldn't keep revolving around Mary. The Mother Earth Plant Shop folded just as abruptly as it had opened. Our unrealistic expectations of living off of the shop's modest income came to a harsh reality within six months. And a combination of the competition from the local grocery stores and Bonnie's discovery that she didn't enjoy dealing with the public brought our closing decision to a head. I couldn't manage it by myself and returned to the security of a secretarial position, working full-time for the Intermediate School District on Queen Anne Hill. Rusty was making good money painting houses, but we were getting tired of city life and began putting out feelers for a place in the country.

Rusty and I rented a small cabin on Whidbey Island, only a short walk from the beach.

It was an introduction to a whole new way of living. I became involved with their food co-op, served as a volunteer teacher's aide for an alternative school, and planted my first vegetable garden. The distance from Seattle to Whidbey offered me some respite from Mary. I spoke with her on the phone, but didn't see her for several months.

I felt some relief as Mary had made friends with some of the Burn Unit staff. By late spring, with the help of one of her new friends, she found a small cottage to rent. It was a block from Lake Union and surrounded by fruit trees. Through Seattle Mental Health Institute (SMHI), Mary began outpatient therapy and, according to what she told me during our few phone conversations, was doing quite well.

1976

As Rusty and I settled into our life on Whidbey, Mary's life and mine grew further apart. She didn't have a car and couldn't drive because of her medications. But once in a while we would bring her to Whidbey for a weekend. She enjoyed walks on the beach with me, but never spoke of her depression. Mary would walk with her head down and hair falling in her face, allowing few glimpses of her expressions. I rarely saw her smile, except to speak of Maggie who was eight at the time. When Maggie spent time with Mom and Dad, Mom would write Mary wonderful letters. Mom made a special effort to keep Mary and Maggie connected. Maggie wrote mainly of school and her visits with Gaggi and Bompi, the fond names she gave my parents.

I always felt sad taking Mary back to Seattle. She had grown apart from her new friends. Her adorable cottage near Lake Union was sold by the owner, forcing her to relocate. She moved into a half-way house on Capitol Hill where she knew some of the out-patients from SMHI. The first time I drove Mary to the half-way house I asked her if I could see her new place. She led me down the stairs through two heavily bolted doors. It was a depressing set-up. No carpet, a stark feeling. There was one large smoke-filled room where several people were wandering about aimlessly. She didn't introduce me to anyone. They just stared. To the right was a little kitchen area separated from the large room by a counter. It reminded me of a church fellowship hall without fellowship. Mary's tiny bedroom was off the large room. The walls were bare, a single bed taking up most of the room. All of her belongings were piled in boxes against the wall, with no apparent attempt to make it homey. I made my visit brief. As I walked back out to the street, taking a deep breath of fresh air, I vowed never to return to that location.

∞

Toward the end of the summer, Rusty and I were watching the evening news when a story with an all too familiar scenario captured our attention. A young woman had jumped off the Aurora Street Bridge and was in critical condition at Harborview. Her identity was unknown.

"Call Harborview at such and such a number with any possible leads to the identity of this woman," the newscaster announced.

I had to call.

"I believe the woman who jumped off the bridge may have been my sister."

"Just a minute while I connect you to the nurse in charge."

I was on hold what seemed like forever, my heart beating rapidly.

Finally a voice. "You're calling about the unidentified woman?"

"Yes, my sister has attempted suicide off a bridge before." My voice was trembling. "I think it could be her."

"Any specific scars or birthmarks?" the nurse asked.

"Severe burn scars on her right leg."

"This woman has no scars on her legs, but I appreciate the call."

Just like that. Mary was in critical condition. Then she wasn't. I never told her about that incident. It was too real.

Mary and I continued to grow apart as Rusty's and my life began turning new corners. Mary, Lobo and I each had inherited $5,000 worth of Texaco stock from Gran Walker. I decided to sell mine and invest in property. We looked at property on Whidbey, on Camano Island, and in the foothills of the Cascades. We wanted to take our time and become knowledgeable about house building. Rusty checked books out from the library. I took a log cabin building class, learned how to fell trees, buck them, skid the bark and season the downed logs.

It wasn't until early 1977 that we made an offer on five acres on Camano Island. It was heavily wooded on a ridge-top (view possibility, the realtor told us). The wide variety of trees and spirit-filled land captured our hearts.

We moved from Whidbey to a rental house in Lynnwood, north of Seattle, while we went through the closing process and prepared to build our dream home. I found an excellent teacher's aide position with Cedar Way Elementary in the Edmonds School District. I had temporarily let go of Mary's problems and felt my life was headed in the right direction.

∞

Buffalo, 1994

KARLA SAT there patiently listening to me ramble throughout our entire meal. The wine was gone, the pasta salad had disappeared, and I was sipping coffee when I realized my need for my old friend's ear had completely taken over our luncheon date. She always took such a keen interest in my life. I often teased her that there must be an issue in her life that she was avoiding in order to keep pursuing the nitty gritty of mine! There was. She acknowledged that she still held onto the pain of losing her father, but wasn't ready to talk about it.

The waitress brought us the bill which we divided equally. Karla had tons more money than I, but she knew how important it was for me to carry my own weight. And for a change, I didn't carry on about Tom's and my depressing financial situation. We hugged and kissed, and Karla agreed to see her therapist about her father before I returned to Buffalo again. I had promised to visit once a year. Once a year I could count on sharing my heart with Karla. The 3,000 mile separation wasn't going to impact our relationship like it would Dad's and mine. Dad had grown accustomed to, and I imagine dependent upon, my periodic weekend visits throughout the year.

I drove back to Dad's apartment wound up from my lunch with Karla. Dad would be waiting for me. I need a plan, I thought. I need to figure out how to gently discuss my upcoming move to Seattle. Dad didn't seem to understand why I had left the east coast in 1973. I was twenty-three then. How could I expect him to understand when I was in my forties? I had four days left of my week-long trip. I had to get through to him. I loved the west and wanted him to understand that I no longer belonged in or around Buffalo. And most importantly, I wanted Dad to understand that I was sorry I would be living so far away from him.

Tomorrow would be it. Tomorrow Dad and I would spend the day at the beach house where I spent so many of my happiest childhood days. Maybe Thunder Bay, the colony in which our summer house stood, would be the catalyst for my special reunion with Dad.

"First things first," Mom would say. First I needed to concentrate on tonight. Tonight, I thought, I get to spend the evening and the whole night at Maggie's apartment. I imagined our evening would be emotional. Maggie was approaching the age of twenty-eight, the same age her mother was when she died. Unlike Mary, Maggie expressed her feelings well. I knew I would be forthright if she asked me the hard questions about Mary's death.

THIRTEEN

Long Night

THE LONG narrow stairway to Maggie's third floor studio apartment seemed much longer than it had two days previously when I first arrived. This time I was alone and nervous. My intuitive side has always been both an asset and a curse. I knew she would want to talk about Mary. I knew I would have to relive the painful memories and tell her the story as I remember it. Much of it had been buried, but I was certain it all would surface once I started recollecting.

The smell of garlic permeated through the hall door. I consciously took a deep breath and rolled my shoulders back. Maggie and I loved each other; there was no reason to be afraid. I knocked. She swung the door open and greeted me with the sweetest smile. Unlike the first afternoon, her apartment had been straightened up, colorful cut up veggies adorned the kitchen counter ready to toss into a stir fry, and steam from the brown rice warmed the air. It was evident that she was excited to show off her new apartment and make me a special dinner.

Filled with her artistic and caring touches, her apartment personified the love and warmth she generates. A beautifully compassionate young woman, her facial characteristics and physical poise are equal to the beauty that haunted her mother. As they did to Mary, well-meaning people tell her how extraordinarily beautiful she is. In my protective manner, I repeatedly remind Maggie about her inner beauty. I don't believe Mary heard that enough.

That night Maggie shared not only about her current self, but dozens of slides from when she was a baby. In the pictures, Mary was her old poised self, radiant with a mother's love for a newborn baby. The slides made me cry.

"Don't cry," Maggie said so sweetly. "I know I'll cry if you keep crying and I don't want tonight to be sad."

"I'm sorry. It's hard for me to see these happy photos of Mary and not think about what could have been."

"Maybe we *should* talk about her." Maggie relinquished. "You never have told me about when she actually died." It had been seventeen years. Maggie seemed ready to hear the story of her mother's tragedy.

I told her how hard it was to be open about Mary's suicide. "You already know Gaggi and Bompi never wanted to talk about Mary's death, right?" Maggie nodded while I continued. "I've always felt so alone with her suicide. A part of me died then and I'll never be the same. It's so sad, but just as it was for Nolie with her Mom, I think it's important for you to hear the story." I was ready.

I began my long and painful account.

∽

Seattle - May, 1977

SPRING WAS in full force with flowers blooming everywhere, a gorgeous warm, sunny morning. The second graders were going to be thrilled with our field trip, a visit to the Ballard Locks. I hadn't seen locks since I was young, probably when I, too, was in second grade. Once we got there, it was I who was the most thrilled; I was the biggest kid of all. In awe of the water level rising and lowering, and the salmon swimming up the ladder, I felt alive. God had given me this day, maybe to remind me what children see so easily, the small wonders of life. Sharing my excitement with the children felt so right, my gift to them, to myself.

Many field trips lose their wonder on the noisy bus ride back to school. This day was different. I held on to that magic as I walked out the school door at the end of the day.

With my spirits high, I decided to visit Mary. I always needed to get psyched for a visit with her since she was usually depressed. It had been a few weeks since the dedication ceremony of our property when she joined us on Camano. She did well at our celebration, but, as always, I could feel her heavy presence. Oh, how I wished I could lift that weight off her shoulders. I wanted to help her, but she never seemed receptive.

Today could be different, I thought. Maybe she's feeling the same warmth of the sun and promise of spring that radiates within me. I headed to Mary's apartment on Capitol Hill, ready to share my high-spirited energy. I was eager to return to Capitol Hill. It reminded me of the days when Rusty and I first came to Seattle. It was a lively place, with young adults going about their carefree lives.

Mary had lived in several apartments between Lake Union and Capitol Hill, the heart of Seattle. This one was her brightest. She had a studio apartment overlooking downtown Seattle, with a view of the Space Needle from her living room window. The western sky lit up the whole apartment, adding life to Mary's space. The room was cheerful, with lush plants hanging in the window. There was no comparison between her new space and her old dark basement apartment with bars on the windows where she'd lived before her tragic jump, or the stark half-way house after the Lake Union cottage was sold. She now seemed to be coming out of her dark days, recovering from her jump off the Roanoke Street Bridge. Thank God that's behind us, always including myself with her problems, I thought to myself as I rang the door bell.

Mary just stared at me when she opened the door. No "Hi Lorn," just a frown on her face. Immediately I sensed she wasn't happy. She started right in.

"I just got off the phone with Daddy. I'm so pissed. He says we're all in the same boat and he won't send me any money." Mary was clearly furious as she led me into the living room.

Same boat, I thought. "I can relate," I said. I told her my sob story. "Rusty and I were broken into last week. Someone stole my camera, our chain saw and our speakers. They probably would've taken the stereo, too, except I think they were scared away." I told her this thinking she'd realize that we really are all in the same boat.

Mary seemed interested in hearing more and began rolling a joint.

Pushing myself up from the comfy couch, I headed to the kitchen for some water, figuring I'd be there a while. The smell of miso soup, onions and brown rice permeated the tiny kitchen. At least Mary was eating well, I thought.

The full bodied fumes of marijuana smoke now filled the living-room as Mary reached her arm toward me when I approached the couch, passing me the joint. As we toked back and forth, I told her about the camera. "There was a whole roll of film still in the camera. Some of the pictures were of the old trees on our property, the ones we had to take down for the house site. The trees are gone now and the photos are gone, too. It makes me sick."

Mary was still preoccupied with her call to Dad and returned to her anger toward him. "He said they had to buy a new furnace and that they couldn't spare any money. That's bullshit," she concluded.

I didn't stop to think that by defending Dad, I would make her more furious. "Maybe they do have plenty of money," I went on, "but he's right that we're all in the same boat. Everyone has different problems; we all have some sort of trials to deal with. Look at what Rusty and I are dealing with. We can't afford to have all that stuff stolen."

I had pushed the button. Mary retaliated with her deep-rooted anger at all the money Mom and Dad seemed to have, especially since Gran and Grandaddy died.

"You don't get it." She spoke with fury. "They have a ton of money and they won't share it with me."

Maybe I don't get it, I thought. I had no clue how much money Mom and Dad had. I had always been independent and earned my own money.

"Don't you get S.S.I. (supplemental security income) benefits?" I pursued.

"Yeah, but that doesn't cover all my expenses," Mary said.

"But Dad gives you a monthly allowance, too, doesn't he?" I had known from when she was living with Rusty and me that Mom and Dad still paid her way and was stupid to enter into that sore subject. I had never gotten a monthly allowance since I had been living on my own, and couldn't conceive of still having that attachment to Mom and Dad.

Mary didn't want to get into the allowance issue or how she was handling her expenses. It was obvious she had enough money to buy grass. I decided not to offer to bale her out and asked what Mom thought about sending money.

"Mom wasn't home. I'm sure she would've offered to help me." Mary knew Mom would do anything to help keep her going. She and Mom were tight. Mom was the liaison between Mary and Maggie, who was living with her father and stepmother. But Mary's relationship with Dad was different. The issue about money ran deep between them.

I remembered one huge blow-out about money. It was about two and a half years earlier, Christmas, 1974, when Mom and Dad came to visit in Seattle. Mary's counselor scheduled an appointment for the whole family. Lobo was there, too. I can see all five of us getting off the elevator at Harborview and following this man into a conference room. We weren't in there long when Mary and Dad starting exploding.

"How much money do you have?" Mary asked him point blank.

"It's none of your business," Dad told her.

Oh God. Here we go, I thought.

She pursued the issue of being family, of being his daughter. "Is it because I'm adopted you won't tell me?" Mary went on. "I suppose Lornie knows how much money you have."

I butted in. "I have no idea."

Dad's face was red. I'm sure his blood pressure was skyrocketing. The counselor decided he needed to talk with Mary alone and excused the rest of us. That was the extent of counseling that Mom, Dad or Lobo ever had.

Clearly nothing had changed since that Christmas of '74. Sitting in Mary's apartment that sunny day in 1977, we went back and forth about Dad and his money, and it was obvious that we weren't about to agree. She yelled at me for defending Dad. I yelled back.

"If you're going to treat me this way when I come for a visit, forget it. I'm not going to come." I stood up and told her that if she wanted me to come again, she could call me.

"You don't have a phone, or have you forgotten?" Mary was one up on me. Rusty and I had decided not to get a phone since we'd be in our rental house for only a few months before our big move to the Camano property.

"All right, drop me a note then," I said. It was absurd for me to expect her to listen to me, but I was too naive and hadn't learned not to triangulate myself by playing the role of the rescuer. I wanted to help her but I didn't know how.

I headed for the door. Mary stayed on the couch. As I opened the door, I turned toward the living room, out of sight from Mary, and said, "I love you."

"I love you, too," Mary dittoed.

I never saw her again.

Driving home, I was furious at myself. My internal dialog wouldn't shut off. I was trying to help, but my defensiveness just seemed to make it worse. Only Mom seemed to understand her, but Mom was 3,000 miles away. I had figured out how to make it financially. Mary hadn't. She was unable to get Dad or me to understand the money part from her perspective. I think Mom understood. She knew hardship. But she also knew perseverance, which Mary hadn't figured out.

I cried all the way home. I had seen Mary in these spirits before and I had an uneasy feeling that she would attempt suicide again. When Rusty came home I told him about my horrible visit with Mary.

"She's going to try to kill herself again, I know it," I cried. He offered no consoling words. My magical day at the Ballard Locks and feeling like a kid again were gone.

∞

Memorial Day Weekend, 1977

As RUSTY and I moved toward making our dream home a reality, we realized it would be best to live on the property while we built the house. Hyde and Cabby Tennis, whom we had kept in touch with since the Roanoke Street Bridge incident, offered to lend us their camper trailer. We borrowed a truck with a trailer hitch from an old Buffalo friend Paula. Paula offered to ride with us when we drove to the Tennis' summer home on Whidbey Island to pick up their camper.

In the truck on that sunny Memorial Day weekend, Paula asked after Mary. It had been over two weeks since I had seen my sister. Paula had known Mary for a long time. She had known her during her debutante days in Buffalo. She had known her through her divorce. And now in Seattle, she had seen Mary many times. She knew of Mary's suicide attempts and was one person I felt I could confide in. As we got off the ferry and headed north on Whidbey, I began telling Paula about my last visit with Mary.

"I'm not feeling good about her," I said and proceeded to tell her the whole ordeal. "I'm worried that she's going to try to kill herself again. I really ought to go see how she's doing, or at least give her a call, but it's always so depressing."

Paula understood and felt badly, too. "*I* should go see her," Paula began, "but I get tired of always being the one to call her."

"That's exactly how I feel," I went on. "I'm tired of putting out all my energy and feeling nothing but her ungratefulness. I hope she's OK. Rusty and I don't have a phone so she can't call me."

I was worried and Paula was, too. She offered some comfort. "If Mary's in need, she can always call *me*."

That put my mind at ease a little. That's right, I thought, Mary could call Paula, trying not to feel so responsible. I took a deep breath and let it go for that day.

∞

THE LAST week of school arrived as Rusty and I packed up the house and prepared to put a ton of belongings into storage getting ready for our big move to the property. We were psyched. We had spent every weekend since the first of April clearing the building site, preparing for a vegetable garden, and learning all about building a house.

Tomorrow is the last day of school, I thought. I promised my class we would have a party and games. They would be dismissed at noon, and I would join the staff for the end-of-the-year luncheon. Most of the staff knew I was searching for a teaching position near Camano so I wouldn't have to face a long commute in the fall. There was sadness in my heart, anticipating what might be my last time with the staff at Cedar Way Elementary. But the promise of a new life on Camano and the excitement of building my own home sustained me.

Rusty and I went to the laundromat to do one final load before our big move. Rain had been coming down all day but let up as we loaded the clean clothes into the van. There was a break in the sky and we became hopeful that the rain would hold off for moving day. As we carried the laundry to the house, I could see a note on our door.

It was a small piece of scrap paper with a phone number and a note saying, "Call us, Hyde and Cabby."

My heart sank. I turned to Rusty. "Mary's dead. I know it."

I can't remember if Rusty said anything. I know he didn't offer any words of comfort. What was there to say? We both knew there was no other reason why Cabby and Hyde would come all the way up to Lynnwood. We decided to get to a phone immediately. We hopped back into the van and headed up to the gas station. Traffic was going by as I dialed from the pay phone.

"Hello," Hyde answered.

"It's Lornie."

She provided no cushion. "Mary's dead," she said, as simple as that, no delaying the inevitable.

"It's over," I mumbled. I can't believe how calm I must have sounded. She had to kill herself. I knew it. We all knew it. But now it was real. I started throwing out questions. "Do Mom and Dad know?" They did.

Hyde went on to tell me the gruesome details.

Mary had jumped off a different, yet higher bridge in Seattle. The 12th Avenue Bridge rose high above Interstate 90 and Dearborn Street, just off I-5. She had no identification on her and had been lying in the city morgue for three weeks. Nameless. Nameless at death, just as she'd been nameless at birth before Mom and Dad adopted her.

Mary had died within a week after I last saw her. Bulletins describing my sister had been put up in mental health clinics all over Seattle. One of Mary's outpatient therapists from SMHI recognized the description and called in with Mom and Dad's phone number. When the mortician called Buffalo, it was Margit who answered the phone at 19 Argyle. Margit had come to polish silver and iron Dad's shirts while Mom was out for the day. Margit who, with her thrifty Norwegian background, would darn my grandfather's socks (light bulb in the heel) and iron the used Christmas wrappings to reuse for another season. Margit who was there the day Mary slit her ankle, finding her in her childhood bed in a pool of blood. Margit was told that it was crucial to contact Mr. or Mrs. Walker. I don't know whether she knew then that Mary had died. She gave the gentleman Dad's work number. On June 10, 1977, in his office, Dad received the call. I can't begin to presume his reaction. But when he was told that someone needed to identify the body, Dad protected me. He asked that Cabby be the one to do it. Cabby had done so prior to driving out to Lynnwood with the news for me.

∞

IT WOULD be twenty years before I learned that identifying Mary's body was one of the most difficult things Cabby had done as a young priest. He told me that it was extremely hard to look at her. He had taken a colleague along for support. He had never had to identify a body before then. After all those years, I had a new appreciation for Cabby, as well as for Dad in sparing me that horrendous task.

On that June evening of 1977, I wanted to call Mom and Dad, but Hyde reminded me that it was close to midnight their time. I didn't sleep that night. I lay in bed tossing and turning, wrestling with the idea that Mary was actually dead. And I was anxious about how I was going to deal with school. It was the last day and would end by 11:30 a.m.; I felt that I couldn't call in sick. By 5:00 a.m., with all the arrangements to take care of stirring in my head, the adrenaline kicked in. In high gear I pulled together as the strong child, attempting to manage this traumatic ordeal, as Mom and Dad would expect. I rolled out of bed and headed for the gas station to call Buffalo. It was shortly after 8:00 a.m., Eastern Standard Time, when Mom answered.

"Mom?"

"Mary's dead," she responded, just as Hyde had.

"I know. I spoke with Hyde last night. I still can't believe it." Poor Mom, I thought. All those years she had held Mary, lying beside her at night, listening to her sorrow and trying to make her life OK. I can imagine Mom thinking, "All for naught."

I assured Mom that everything was under control at this end. "I'm meeting Hyde this afternoon to make the cremation arrangements. Today's my last day of teaching. I have to go in this morning because I promised the kids a party. Then I'll meet Hyde at Mary's apartment to notify her manager." All this was probably blowing right over Mom's head. She called me Mary. I didn't correct her. She had just lost her daughter, the daughter she had spent twenty-eight years trying to convince she loved.

"I sent a telegram to Lobo," Mom said. We didn't have his phone number. I presumed it helped him keep his distance from Buffalo. All we had was a post office box number. "Hopefully, he'll check his mail in time to make it for the service," she continued.

All three of us West Coast "kids" were far from Mom and Dad's reach, and now they would have to bury one, find another, and depend on the third. I took a deep breath, feeling the weight on my shoulders. No time to cry.

"Do you know when you'll have the service?" I was in disbelief of how fast this was happening.

"We've tentatively set it for Tuesday, presuming you can make it home in time."

"I'll call the airlines as soon as I can."

The whole conversation seemed surreal. Mary was actually dead. It was over now. Or was it?

There was Maggie. Maggie was only nine. How do you tell a nine-year-old that her mother is dead? That her mother has taken her own life?

"Have you told Maggie?" I continued.

"That's Dan's job," she told me. "Dan's her father; he's raising her. I told him he must tell Maggie."

"Good for you," I reinforced her. "Mom, I still have to take a shower and get ready for work. I'll call later this afternoon."

"OK. We love you."

"I love you, too," I said, and then she was gone.

What an aching pain Mom must have felt. But I imagine, just as

I did, she buried it and conjured up her inner strength to hide her pain and deal with the plans that needed to be made.

∽

THE MANAGER of Mary's building was more than willing to let Hyde and me into Mary's place. He told us she was behind on her rent and that he hadn't seen her and was beginning to worry about her. He waived the rent and told us that whatever we left behind would be donated to the Salvation Army.

Her apartment had lost its warmth. The sun was shining, but the life was gone. The plants were drooping, uncared for. Mary's bed was unmade and dirty clothes were strewn all over the floor. The kitchen sink was piled with dirty dishes. The stove had a crusty old pan sitting on top, old miso soup, I thought. Tears welled up when I remembered the great smells from my last visit, envisioning Mary's love for brown rice and miso soup. Hyde and I began digging into the chore of cleaning things up and figuring out what to save. There wasn't much, besides a few knickknacks, a mattress, an old Goodwill sofa, some small tables and old clothes. The stereo was the only valuable belonging. And more valuable than it seemed. She had once told me that the radio was her best friend. How lonely she must have been to consider the radio her best friend. I boxed up her stereo and a pair of white overalls that I could remember Mary wearing. She also had a pile of journals which I set aside to save. I certainly couldn't deal with them then.

Hyde was my rock that day. She led me from one necessary step to another. From Mary's apartment we headed to the funeral home, Bonney Watson. I had driven by that place countless times during my first years in Seattle. Now I would learn what the inside was like. Why me? Why did I have to go through this? I was twenty-seven and wanted to live an "adult life," but I didn't want this. Later, the funeral director wrote a letter to Mom and Dad telling them what a wonderful job their daughter did arranging for Mary's cremation. I wish I could have felt the same. He didn't have to see me fall apart on the plane to Buffalo, the 3,000 mile plane ride during which I carried Mary's ashes on my lap, the longest plane ride of my life.

It was a red-eye flight from Seattle to New York City. Then I would make a connection on to Buffalo. I was exhausted. The flight was full. The stewardess did her usual spiel about putting all carry-on luggage under the seat in front of you. I looked at the box of ashes that I had been holding onto for dear life and thought, no way is this leaving my lap. I'll treat it as though it's my purse, knowing everyone gets to hold onto their purse during take-off. The plane took off and I tried to ignore the six-inch square cardboard shipping box I was carrying on my lap. Instead, I focused on the past two days which had gone by so quickly.

As I remembered my last day at school, I mused about my use of the word "predicament," remembering how Mom had used it when Nolie's Dad died, and then how I had used it myself.

When I walked into the school office that last morning, I told the secretary that I was in a predicament and needed to meet with the principal. My principal passed through the office just then and asked what I wanted.

"Lornie has a predicament," the secretary said.

I told him I needed to talk with him privately. After he closed his office door and told me to have a seat, I said, "It's really more than a predicament. Last night I learned that my sister has died."

Usually he didn't make eye contact, which had bothered me in my initial interview. This time, he looked right at me and told me he was sorry. "Was it expected?" he asked.

Not allowing any emotion, I was forthright. "It was a suicide. She had tried several times before." I felt no need to tell him that she had already been dead for three weeks and got right into my immediate needs. "As soon as the kids are dismissed, I'll have to leave to handle the funeral arrangements. I'm sorry to miss out on the staff luncheon."

He assured me that I could leave right then if I wished, but I told him that I wanted to keep my promise to the class and give them their party. I guess it was in my blood not to let emotions come before duty.

I should have been nominated for an Academy Award for my performance that day. No one had a clue that my inner self was screaming. I couldn't bring myself to share my tragic news with any of the staff, not even Ward, a fourth grade teacher who had become my one good friend at Cedar Way.

I wanted to appear strong and decided to attend the luncheon since I might not be returning in the fall. But by the time lunch was served, my strong facade couldn't be held up any longer. I didn't have the kids to give me strength as I did earlier that morning. I didn't allow myself to cry or let down, but I knew I couldn't make small talk any longer. I excused myself early and told those sitting next to me, including Ward, that I had a meeting to attend.

Some meeting. Meeting with Mary's apartment manager. Meeting with the funeral director. Meeting with Hyde and Cabby for cocktails. Hell. I had several meetings to attend! What a day, I thought. And how I chose the word predicament. Predicament. Thirteen years after learning the meaning of that word, I did it. I used it correctly. Me, Lornie Walker, the slow learner, the klutz, the one who had no self-esteem. I even checked Webster's definition to reinforce myself. It was no wonder I had to double check my knowledge. As a child, I had had a horrible time learning how to read and felt it would never happen. As I had struggled with work at school, my low self-esteem became more pronounced. I can still remember the people in my slow readers' group. Almost forty years later I remember Robbie Folsom, Diana Rogers, Carl Smith and Melissa

Frank. It makes me cry to think about us. We five always stood out from the others. We knew we were different. I felt that I'd never be able to make something of my life. From third through twelfth grade I went to a great private school with an excellent student/ teacher ratio, and yet I wasn't making any progress. Mom and Dad decided to send me to Mrs. Priebe, a reading specialist. I was eight or nine and remember the simple screening tests, which required looking at photographs with some kind of inconsistency, a picture of a girl carrying an opened umbrella on a sunny day, or a girl walking a duck on a leash while a dog swam in a tiny nearby pond.

I can see the table where Mrs. Priebe laid down three little square cardboard photos for me to sequence—a child going down a slide, a child climbing the slide ladder, and one photo of the child landing on her butt. I liked visuals. But teachers weren't into figuring out different learning styles back then. Instead, Mrs. Priebe led me into a small dark room, with no distractions, to read to her. I remember having the creeps. Her house was too quiet, too dark and too plain. I sat at a work table with nothing but a small desk lamp and read a stupid book to her. She asked a bunch of questions I couldn't answer. Over and over I would read sentence after same sentence until I could answer her questions. I felt stupid.

∞

COCKTAILS WITH Hyde and Cabby helped. The wine they offered helped me slow down and breathe a little. I knew it would. I remember feeling as though I were in Buffalo. It was comforting, as though I was on Argyle Park. After I had moved to D.C., Hyde and Cabby bought the Stryker's house. They had become close friends with Mom and Dad. They knew Nolie's history, they knew mine, and most significantly, they knew Mary's. Their presence gave me a sense of security. They sat by me as I made my plane reservations and as I arranged to pick up Mary's ashes. They were there when I called Mom and Dad to finalize my plans to return to Buffalo and bring Mary home one last time. Mary.

On the plane, I was caught off guard when I looked down and the reality of holding Mary's remains began to sink in. My strength crumbled and I began to sob. The box seemed heartlessly cold. Such a harsh way to maintain the remains of a human being. I began loosening my tight grip on the box. Sitting between two strangers, I felt miniscule and alone. I had no intention of opening up to the man by the window, but felt a temptation to speak to the woman on my right. A woman would be more sympathetic, I imagined. She must've noticed I was crying. I didn't approach the woman and remained feeling helplessly alone. Again, I looked down at the plain box. The container which held Mary's ashes was a mystery to me. It had been packaged within a shipping box with her name and an identification number in the corner. My sister, my beautiful sister, was condensed into this small box. Her whole life wrapped up into one small package. Faceless. But not to me.

I closed my eyes and let images of Mary flow through my mind, the nine-year-old Mary standing next to me in our matching Easter outfits, and another photo, my favorite, of the same vintage, probably taken at St. Paul's, with Mary and me holding hands in our dress coats with velvet collars. And as though it were yesterday, I could see Mary and Dad. Hand in hand, they marched up onto the platform for the dress rehearsal of the debutante ball. Mary was wearing an old checkered dress and a bandana, not very elegant, but on her, everything looked beautiful. Beauty. One of Mary's greatest obstacles, I thought. I reached down to my day pack and pulled out my journal, thinking this small plain box held all that was left of Mary.

So many thoughts raced through my mind as I prepared to take Mary home for the last time. I wrote until my entire being couldn't handle any more. I swallowed my tears with as little sound as possible. I was afraid of disturbing my seat mates. They had fallen asleep and the entire plane was dark and quiet. All except the little light over my head. I reached up high and switched off the light.

FOURTEEN

Aftermath

L OBO DIDN'T make it for the funeral. It was just the three of us.
The sermon and music were a blur. The only clear image I have
is of the organist playing the recessional hymn to a packed church.
I walked slowly out of the Cathedral with Mom and Dad arm in
arm on either side of me, past hundreds of family friends who were
there to support us. In a receiving line outside the church doors,
people I hadn't seen in several years shook our hands and gave us
hugs. There was no mention of Mary, only greetings of "good to see
you, Lornie."

*At the time, I didn't know what to make of their reactions, or lack
thereof. For years I didn't know what to make of Mary's death. Mom
said Mary was better off and there was no need to talk about 'it.' So,
we didn't.*

*I believe Dad took Mary's death the hardest. Similar to me, he was
carrying years of unresolved stuff between himself and Mary. He buried
all of his thoughts and began living in a shell. I didn't try talking to*

either Mom or Dad about the emotional effects of Mary's death until almost a year later. That's when Mom reminded me that I was too analytical and needed to put Mary behind me. Mom's words always stung. No one wanted to talk about it. Suicide is considered a disgrace to one's family. Our collective guilt, anger and sadness became deeply buried.

After a week with Mom and Dad, I flew back to Seattle and moved into the tiny camper that Rusty and I had borrowed from the Tennis'. Lobo finally reached Mom and Dad a few days after the funeral. He decided to wait and fly to Buffalo a few weeks later.

Rusty and our property became my focus. By day, Rusty and I worked on the property preparing the foundation and scrounging old job sites for recycled lumber. By night, he'd drink and I'd smoke pot. Rusty wasn't good at expressing himself emotionally. I shut down, feeling alone with my guilt.

That fall, unable to find a teacher's aide job in Camano Island's school system, I carpooled with other teachers and made the long daily trek to Edmonds, returning to another year at Cedar Way. My long days commuting and Rusty's long hours on the house began taking a toll on our relationship. We poured ourselves into the house on the weekends and made no time for each other.

The following spring, March of '78, we moved into the house. We limped along, enabling each other with our altered states of mind. I loved Rusty and didn't want to live without him. He meant no harm with his drinking and was never abusive, just as I meant no harm with my smoking. We had been together for six years, longer than most of our friends' relationships had lasted. But that summer I discovered he had slept with someone else and I couldn't find it in my heart to forgive him.

We tried a few counseling sessions, but Rusty wouldn't consider making a marital commitment. I wanted a family and wasn't willing to be an unwed mother, especially as a teacher within the public school system. I asked Rusty to move out in December of '78. Signing an agreement, we treated our break up as though it were a divorce. He took the dogs, TV and stereo. I kept the house and made monthly payments to Rusty for his labor on the house building. The property was mine.

That same winter I finally landed a job as a teacher's aide at the local Stanwood Elementary school and began feeling part of the community. I became certain that my life was going to turn around now that Rusty and I had separated. I was convinced that it was he who had brought me down and now my old spirit would return. I was wrong.

Over the next couple of years my involvement within the community grew—organizing entertainment for local fairs, emceeing talent shows and earning respect in the public eye. During the day, the children I worked with became the light of my life, but my personal life was in shambles. The demanding maintenance of the house intensified my loneliness and I was smoking and drinking more than I care to remember.

My community presence was just a facade for a person who was tearing apart inside. I was fooling myself. Gradually, I knew Mary's suicide was eating at me. I tried therapy and started attending prayer breakfasts. In therapy, I re-enacted scenes from childhood, role playing myself and role playing Mary. I wasn't sure who I was anymore. It was a combination of therapy and the prayer breakfasts, that became my initial path toward healing. I felt unconditional support from a few women in the prayer group whom I worked with daily at Stanwood Elementary. They were older women whose faith reminded me of Mom's. They surrounded me during my working hours, invited me to retreats, and made sure I felt included in the monthly prayer groups.

They became my angels.

I was asked to be a speaker for one of the prayer breakfasts, to tell about myself and my faith. I ended up focusing my talk on the devastating effects of Mary's suicide.

In preparing my message for the prayer group, I began to realize the impact Mary's death had on me and how I had lost perspective of my own life. I was able to compare my loneliness to hers and recognize my fear. If I allowed myself to continue feeling alone and escape in an unhealthy way, I would end up like Mary. The support of 'my angels' helped renew my faith.

I realized much later that who I thought I was, was based on how I saw myself in comparison to Mary and how Mary herself saw me. I couldn't allow myself to shine. Once she died, I had no one to compare myself to. Somewhat like an adolescent trying to fit into the adult world, I needed to feel my way back into society and learn how I fit into this rapidly changing world.

FIFTEEN

Thunder Bay

M Y EVENING with Maggie was long and draining. I'm not sure exactly how much I told her and how much I relived after going to bed. We got up early as I had warned Maggie I needed to pick up Dad and get to the beach by noon. I had a big day lined up at Thunder Bay, our family's summer home.

She hemmed and hawed about possibly going herself.

"I'm planning to cook dinner for Dad, Lobo and, possibly, Isabel," I told her. Isabel was Lobo's girlfriend. "You're welcome, too." I knew Maggie and Isabel had never hit it off, but I truly hoped she'd consider joining us for dinner.

"Isabel's coming?" Maggie asked disappointedly.

"Lobo wasn't sure. She might," I continued.

"Lornie, I don't trust that woman. In fact, Bompi hasn't been too sweet to me either, lately."

Dad's heartwarming love for Maggie had taken a turn during the past year. She and I believed it was related to his repressed anger toward Mary, displacing it on Maggie. And Lobo felt caught in the middle between Isabel and Maggie. Poor Lobo. Finally, he had found a woman who seemed to change his life, to give him a reason for living and he couldn't find acceptance of her by his family. And here I was desperately trying to find my place in the family, feel loved by Dad, and move across the continent feeling comfortable about leaving my family behind.

The delicious soy and granola cereal Maggie poured for us that morning was another sign of the healthy life she was trying to lead. Her kitchen was graced with fresh fruit, a juicer and herbal teas. She spoke as I was sipping my tea. "I'm not going to let Isabel keep me from enjoying Thunder Bay. I'm going." Maggie was determined!

"All right!" I seemed energized by this challenge. "You and I can balance her domineering energy." Look out, I thought to myself.

∞

THUNDER BAY was the epitome of every child's dream. Pristine sandy beaches lined a small inlet on Lake Erie where the warm summer water would gradually deepen between sandbars, forming the most idyllic swimming area. Thunder Bay Colony consisted of privileged American families who owned waterfront property along the Canadian lake shore.

As a child, I was unaware of the exclusivity of the colony to which our beach home belonged. In my own safe world, listening to crickets and the sound of distant trains during the night, I knew of no other child who didn't share the same experience. We were a cloister, a group of families closed off from the rest of the world from June through Labor Day.

Thunder Bay, two words that summarized my summers. We didn't go on summer vacations. We went to Thunder Bay, where fourteen other families joined their resources to build three private tennis courts, provide a wide array of Fourth of July fireworks, and offer swimming, sailing and tennis lessons to their children. I always loved going to Thunder Bay. They were fun filled, safe and secure days, days I wish that all children could experience.

Every year for Mother's Day, Mom, Dad, Lobo, Mary and I would spend most of the weekend at Thunder Bay preparing for the summer months. We would hose down the large picture windows overlooking Lake Erie, the windows we would sit behind during the summer, watching the most incredible light shows as the thunder storms swept across Lake Erie. Those windows also provided the most beautiful view of colored sails during the summer boat races.

On Mother's Day weekend, we would drag the porch furniture from the back bedrooms and place them in their designated area, according to Mom as she directed her crew. The furnace would be turned down as we opened the doors and windows allowing the spring air to fill the house. We tossed the mouse traps, shook out the rugs, swept and mopped the floors, bringing new life back to our favorite house.

Memorial Day weekend marked the beginning of summer for us as we packed our old Country Squire station wagon full of extra kitchen ware, linens, our small portable TV and summer clothes. If we didn't "officially" move over that weekend, we would stay weekends until school let out for the summer.

It was a short jaunt from one cloistered world to another. Thunder Bay is only a twenty minute drive from Buffalo. The drive crossed the Niagara River on the Peace Bridge, through long lines at Canadian Customs, which could sometimes add another twenty minutes. We always had to be prepared for the questions at Customs. Where were you born? How long will you be in Canada? Do you have anything to declare? From as early as I can remember, Mom and Dad used to smuggle their gin and whiskey across the border. We would keep straight faces as Dad would answer "not a thing" to the last question. Over the years, summer residents, the same people who were members of The Saturn Club, got caught at the Peace Bridge, putting a stop to most of the smuggling.

Hired help and summer attire were part of the pretentiousness I grew to abhor—tennis whites for the courts, Lily dresses and Pappagallo shoes for the patio cocktail parties, and school girls (our name for nannies) for the little ones. And now I was returning. I still loved Thunder Bay, even though the exclusivity had become obvious to me. It represented a part of my childhood which I was so fond of. The part of my world which still seemed unbroken.

The house had changed though. It had changed since Mom died. Isabel had been leaving her imprint. And I was still getting used to Mom's absence while trying to accept Isabel's presence.

∞

I LEFT Maggie's apartment and decided to take a walk to clear my head. Both the draining night and the anticipation of the trip to Thunder Bay were getting the better of me. As I strolled down Elmwood Ave. and passed Buffalo State College, I started to smile remembering the summer of '84 when I first met Karla and why I had returned to Buffalo then.

∞

Buffalo, 1984

I HAD a meeting in the administrative office at Buffalo State College during my first full year back in school. I could almost taste my teaching degree. After I discussed my transferable credits with an advisor, Karla appeared from behind me, seemingly out of nowhere. My back had been turned to her while I was talking. I turned around and found her staring at me. She laughed as though we were old friends and began talking in her lively New York accent.

"I guess I don't know you, but thought I recognized your voice. Have I heard you on the radio?"

I wondered to myself where this woman was coming from. "I don't think so," I responded, feeling a bit flattered.

"Oh, it doesn't matter," Karla went on. "Are you from Buffalo?"

She seemed genuinely interested in me. I went on to tell her that I grew up in Buffalo, moved to the West Coast in the seventies and had recently returned. She immediately took an interest in my life and couldn't believe I would return to Buffalo by choice!

Return to Buffalo by choice. Karla had pressed *the* button during our first encounter in 1984.

I told her what a hard decision it had been for me to come back. I had been gone for over ten years and wasn't sure what Buffalo could offer me.

"It's a long story, but basically I came back because of my marriage."

I can hear her now. "Oh my god, it's because of my husband that I'm here, too!"

We soon realized we were the same age, newlyweds, teachers and had a zest for life that we wanted to share with each other. During those first years of my marriage and life in Buffalo, Karla became my best friend.

∽

Buffalo, 1982

I HAD returned to Buffalo to marry Tom. It sounds simple, but in actuality, I practically had to be dragged back. Mom had introduced

me to Tom the Christmas of '82. I always tease that we have an arranged marriage. I had sold the Camano house and was attending
Seattle Central Community College at the time, earning credits toward a BA. It was during one of our weekly Sunday afternoon calls
that Mom told me: "We have a new priest at St. Paul's I want you
to meet—don't meet anyone new," she said with such authority. It
had been almost four years since Rusty and I had broken up. I had
dated a few people during those years but had been relationship-free
for a while.

"A priest!" I was floored. "You've got to be kidding!" I can hear
myself responding.

Mom started describing him. "He's not your typical priest. He's
earthy. He lived on an island for awhile. He's a tall, handsome redhead."

"What's his name?" I was curious.

"Tom Craighead. Isn't that a great name?"

"Craighead? I don't know, I've never heard of it."

"It's Scottish, I think it sounds prestigious."

I could see where this was going. "You're not suggesting I marry
a priest, be a clergy spouse? I haven't attended church for more than
ten years." I felt she had gone mad!

"You don't have to marry him. I just thought I'd throw a little
dinner party so you can at least see for yourself."

Mom would have her way, I knew it. "I guess there's no stopping
you, is there?"

"I'll respect your wishes, if you'd rather not meet him."

"No, go ahead, it can't hurt."

I was feeling strong on my own. I had stopped smoking pot.
Seattle Pacific University had just accepted me into their Special
Education Program. I was finally going to get my degree. I had been
living alone for a few years and didn't want to give up my life in Seattle, or my life in Washington, where I knew I belonged. My roots

were in the west now, ten years developing friendships, friends who experienced the changes of the seventies with me and who saw me through Mary's death. They were friends who knew me better than most of those whom I grew up with. It seemed like a conspiracy to get me back into church and Buffalo society, the social world from which I had fled and never really had belonged. I knew I would fight it.

Tom had a good job. Not just any job. He was the Canon of the Cathedral, the assistant to the Dean in the Episcopal Cathedral. Not just any cathedral, but St. Paul's Cathedral, where I was raised. The church with The Walker Room. The pressure would be great if I chose to move back to Buffalo. I would no longer be Lornie Walker. I'd be Bill and Lorna's daughter dating, or possibly marrying, the new canon. The thought made me cringe.

∞

THIS WAS more than a party to celebrate my "coming home" for the holidays. Mom dug up a few old high school friends. "Friends" I hadn't seen in fifteen years! Some of them knew me during my early hippie days and had similar values, but it would be hard to find common ground with the others. And then there was Tom. Mom had told me that she had told him all about me. Knowing Mom's gregariousness, I imagine Tom also knew this was a setup.

Unlike Mary, I had forfeited the debutante life, but that night I felt like the queen of the ball being introduced to the "right" man. I was a nervous wreck before anyone arrived. Not wanting to appear anxious, I stayed upstairs and sat on a twin bed in Mary's old bedroom, strumming my dulcimer. My old bedroom had become Maggie's room. Mary's room was bigger and brighter and I could spread my stuff out more. I tried hard not to think of Mary. Not to think of the tragedy that had taken place in her old room. Was it this bed or the other one where she first tried to take her life, I wondered. Oh God, put her out of your head, Lornie. You can't think about her now.

I played "Simple Gifts," one of my favorite songs, over and over, trying to convince myself, as the words to the song went, I was "in the place just right." The door bell rang as the clock struck six. God, I prayed Tom wouldn't be first. He was. So much for prayer! I came down the front stairs as Mom headed to the door at the same time. Tom was standing in the vestibule which separated us from the cold December night and the warmth of our big old house on Argyle Park. The door to the front hall had an oversized window leaving Tom standing there staring at me as I walked down the stairs, making my grand entrance even more pronounced. Dramatic and almost comical.

Tom's pock-marked, scarred face surprised me, but made him more real. His magnificent magnetic smile was filled with love. His hands hung easily from his long arms. He looked at ease with himself. Mom was right, there was an earthiness about him. That night I witnessed first-hand the tall, handsome, green-eyed redhead with whom Mom had been so enthralled.

I can't remember our initial introduction. We must have grabbed a drink soon after he arrived. Episcopalians are known for their ability to down drinks at cocktail parties! We settled into the living room before any of the other guests arrived. I was not nearly as relaxed as Tom. I didn't sit, or offer him a seat. We were still standing when the other guests started to arrive.

Photographs capturing that special evening show that it was a coat and tie affair, Tom being no exception. I, however, wasn't wearing the attire typically expected of "old" Buffalo. Getting me to wear a dress is almost impossible after all my years of dressing up for church, dancing school and attending my peers' debutante balls. Instead, I wore a folksy green skirt with red and blue trim, a turtleneck sweater and tights. My hair was a different matter. I was going through a drastic hair change after cutting off my long golden locks, which had been ruined by a permanent. It had that ugly in between look when you change from short to long hair.

My hair didn't seem to matter to Tom. He wanted to know me. There were a few things that bonded us immediately, most of which (thanks to Mom) we were aware of before meeting. We both had been involved in anti-war protests in the early seventies (probably attended the same events). Tom had experienced island living off the coast of Maine. I had lived on two islands in Puget Sound. My sister had died at age twenty-eight; his brother, at the time we met, was on his death bed at age twenty-nine. We both seemed to be late bloomers and just now settling into what we really hoped to do with our lives.

Tom and I stayed up long after everyone was gone, and long after Mom and Dad had gone to bed. Sitting on the living room floor at 19 Argyle Park, we shared our pasts, our present, and our dreams. We didn't kiss, but I parted with a clear sense that we could have a future together.

Tom knew I didn't want to leave the west, but our attraction to each other was so strong, there was no stopping me. We were soul mates. Friends often say we look like brother and sister. We weren't young kids anymore. He was thirty-two, I, thirty-three. Both left-handed Pisces born only a year apart, my intuition told me this was it, time for us to settle down and make a life together. Mom was right. Ye Gads! How could my mother be right, choose the man for me to marry? My mother who shared the same name as I? It was a nightmare and a dream in one.

Our luncheon date the next day was the clincher. Tom invited me to his apartment. We both agreed that by going out somewhere public in our small community, we would have no privacy.

Tom had rented an attractive carriage apartment behind one of

Buffalo's estate homes. The Cathedral had set him up well. I followed him up the long stairway, telling him I thought I had been to a debutante party in the main house. I reassured Tom that I hadn't been part of that world. I could hear him let out a sigh of relief.

We continued up the stairs, settled in his large living room, and looked at photos from a year he had spent on an island in Maine. I wished I'd had my island-life photos to share. Instead, I described images of my self-built home on Camano Island, the house I had built with Rusty. He didn't want to hear about Rusty, but was thrilled to learn of the commonalities we both had.

He had left Maine with a new perspective of his life and begun his quest for the priesthood. I, too, had left an island, and gone back to Seattle, in search of my long-awaited special education degree.

This was a long lunch hour. I'm sure we had visited for almost an hour before he led me to the kitchen for lunch. He assured me he didn't need to watch the clock. He asked if I liked spinach salad.

"Yes," I said, but I had no idea what I was in for.

He couldn't find a bowl and dumped the leftover church salad into a large dented pan. With no serving spoons, he reached both of his large hands, hopefully recently washed, into the pan and dished out servings for each of us. Not an ounce of pretentiousness. I knew then he was for me.

∞

Minutes before the St. Paul's Christmas Eve Service began, Tom strolled down the center aisle to one of the front pews where the Walker clan always perched, and handed me a Christmas gift. Just as swiftly and prominently, he turned around and strolled back to prepare for the processional. All eyes were on the new canon and this out-of-town old timer who had "come home." I could have killed him for being so visible.

I tucked the package beside me and figured I'd deal with it later when I wasn't drawing so much attention. I still hadn't opened it when I greeted Tom after the service, but thanked him for what looked like a book.

"My brother's not well at all," Tom told me. "I'll be flying out first thing tomorrow morning."

Christmas day, I thought. "Your family will be glad you're there. Do you need a ride to the airport?" I asked, thinking maybe we could have one more meeting.

"Actually, that'd be great if you could."

We confirmed the time of departure and when I would pick him up.

It was well after midnight on Argyle after the service when I opened the package and read his long inscription in the book, *More Than Wanderers*. "Lornie, As you and I talked, there was this connection for me… In thankfulness for that, in a spirit of friendship, and to your health, I offer this gift and my beset wishes to you on your journey. May God's Peace be with you always, Tom." My heart melted to think how sensitive he was, how considerate. I tossed and turned, too excited for the sun to rise when I would see Tom again.

Christmas morning at the airport we affirmed our mutual desire to continue communicating. We both agreed we were nervous and had never dealt with a long distance relationship, but felt it was worth a try. When Tom's flight number was called, we turned toward each other. His infectious smile and genuine expression seemed to invite me to lean forward with a big hug. As we backed away from the warm hug, he leaned down and kissed me briefly on the lips. I smiled and gave him a peck. In a moment he was out of sight, but the feeling that we were destined to be together kept growing.

I headed back to Seattle a few days later. We wrote, made tape recordings and accrued substantial phone bills. Tom visited me in Seattle and I attended summer classes in Buffalo, testing the strength of our short courtship. From March through June, I went steadily to a therapist, trying to figure out how I could move back to Buffalo and marry a priest my mother had introduced me to.

SIXTEEN

Learning to Forgive

Buffalo, 1994

FINDING MY place in the family was top priority. With Mary and Mom gone, Dad treating Lobo like royalty, and me moving 3,000 miles away, my insecurities continued to be high. Years of therapy and my life experiences were jumbled in my head as I tried to make sense of it all.

Close to twenty years had passed since Mary died. Too many of those years were spent unwilling to let go of the flaws Mary saw in me. The ones she pointed out in her journals, her vision of who I was, which was so painful to read:

Lornie who's trying to straighten me out,
is in reality fucking me over
Lorn - note - fuck off dumb materialist

The latter was written right after our final visit. I'm sure she was referring to my comments about Rusty and me having some of our possessions stolen and Dad's need for a new furnace. I had sided with Dad that we were all in the same boat. Obviously, she felt strongly that we were not. Possibly she was thinking of writing a note to that effect. I'll never know.

On good days, I didn't accept what she wrote, but her strong words were hard to ignore. It was difficult to tell whether her entries were dreams or reality. Sometimes she referenced dreams, but other writings seemed random and appeared to be written in angst. Maybe it was her manic depression taking hold. Maybe she was skipping her meds. These are things I'll never know. I do know I never meant to hurt her. I was naive and felt totally responsible.

If only. If only. If only. I repeated those words for years after she died. If only I hadn't fought with her that last day. If only I had gone back to her apartment a day or two later when I knew she was feeling so desperate. If only I hadn't defended Dad. If only I hadn't introduced her to marijuana.

And the ultimate "if only." If only I hadn't been born. She wouldn't have had to contend with this younger miracle sister. I never saw myself as the miracle baby, the bonus baby Mom always told me that I was. For as long as I can remember, I was the mistake. The baby they thought they could never have. The daughter they hadn't planned. I spent many years trying to be the "good child," trying to prove to Mary that Mom and Dad loved me because I was a good girl, not because I was their natural born. But no matter how hard I tried, she would throw it back when I got off the hook for something. "You love Lornie more because she's your birth child," she'd cry.

∞

JANE, A high school friend of Mary's, wrote to me after Mary died. She was one of the few honest persons willing to write or talk openly about the feelings I struggled with from being raised as the only biological child. She told me it was as though I was born with a germ, the germ of being the only natural child, of being "the legitimate one."

A portion of Jane's letter to me:

You've been in a sensitive position all your life—being the the natural child growing up with two adopted siblings. For that reason alone, I'm sure there were conflicts for Mary. No matter what you might do, how you might behave, or in what manner your parents treated you— there must always have been the germ --"They must love her more."

I believe that much of what you endured over the years in your relationship with Mary was strongly influenced by that. She being resentful/fearful of your "legitimacy" within the family, and your trying to downplay your special position by being good and responsible—not wanting to appear to be rewarded without having earned it.

My two cousins are adopted and even without a natural child in the family, they have had many problems which persist to the present—their origins, their self worth (why were they given away), and fear of abandonment. Under the best of circumstances it is difficult for all of us to feel loved enough, good enough, deserving enough.

Jane was right when she wrote about downplaying my special position by being good and responsible, knowing that Mary was resentful of my legitimacy. I volunteered in my community as a young adult, just as I had done alongside Mom when I was little. I cared deeply about what was going on around me and wanted to make a difference. Mary was wrapped up in herself. She probably resented my ability to cope with the outside world. I've always loved helping in my community, but some of the "perfect Lornie" image that I tried to hold forth for Mom and Dad was probably created to cover up my own inadequacies and make me feel more worthwhile.

I was blind to Mary's fear of abandonment and lack of self-worth. I knew in my heart that outward beauty didn't matter, but my own sense of unworthiness was so predominant, I couldn't see hers. I was too caught up in envying what she had. In elementary and junior high, Mary would have trouble falling asleep. Mom would spend countless evenings reading and cuddling with her until she nodded off. I never got that. I had my teddy bear. Teddy was my security. I would snuggle with Teddy, feeling his soothing soft fur as I drifted off to sleep.

In high school Mary was the light of her English teacher's life. And, painfully, I felt she was Mom's light. I believe that the attention Mom gave Mary was out of pure love. And it was most probably out of that same pure love that Mom presumed I was strong and didn't need her constant reassurance. I enviously watched Mom coddle Mary through mononucleosis during her junior year of high school. Mary spent weeks in her bedroom, never getting dressed, while Mom waited on her hand and foot. It was late winter when Mom decided to fly to Florida with Mary to help her recuperate. They stayed in Fort Lauderdale for over a month.

I didn't feel too resentful at the time because Dad took me to Florida a few weeks later during my spring break. I had recently passed my drivers test and helped Dad drive down the eastern seaboard. It was a rare, one-on-one special time alone with Dad. It makes me laugh to think of the day we departed from Buffalo. We were over an hour south of the city when I remembered that my dress/church clothes for the week were still hanging on my closet door.

Looking back, I believe it was an intentional faux pas, so as not to have to get dressed up. But to Dad, it was precious dollars. Rather than splurging on a couple of new dresses, he turned around, drove all the way home and lost three hours of travel time that first day en route to Florida!

It was long after Mary died when I realized Mary's illness that spring might not have been mono alone, but also the beginning of her long bouts with depression. It was hard for me to accept that she was manic-depressive. I always thought the manic part was a high energy obsessive/compulsive-type behavior. But I learned later it could also be manifested in anger. And Mary certainly spent a lot of her energy wrought up in anger. But even with all the anger she displayed, Mary could live up to the sophisticated society image that Mom had learned to enjoy. She presented that image perfectly, abounding with grace and beauty.

She chose not only the debutante road, but was also chosen to be in the Queen's court following the culminating banquet and dance, the Snow Ball. I couldn't have cared less about being part of that world. We had been given the choice as to whether to be Debs (the nickname for debutantes) or not. If not, we could spend a summer in Europe. I chose Europe. I still had several friends who were Debs and whose parties I attended. The long fancy dresses, of which one needed several different styles, the white gloves, the fancy hair-dos, and the small talk were all part of a world in which I didn't feel comfortable. I couldn't wait to escape Buffalo and avoid the rest of the Deb parties that summer of '67.

But that same summer following Mary's debut, she tricked Mom and Dad with her manipulative skills. No matter how unfair it so blatantly seemed, Mary convinced Mom and Dad that she should go to Europe, too. She and Nolie went alone, traveling through France and Italy. I, as had been planned for over a year, traveled with a chaperoned group from school and studied French while visiting France, Italy and Switzerland.

∞

FORGIVING MARY and Dad has been easier than forgiving myself. I believe neither of them knew what their impacts were or would be. Dad's silence seemed to be out of self-protection. I imagine he could not endure the pain of talking about Mary's problems and death, or the other losses in his life. He didn't seem equipped to deal with those kinds of emotions. Knowing I was moving west was one more unfathomable loss. He didn't want to acknowledge my leaving nor open the old wounds surrounding Mary's death. I accept that now.

Learning how hard it has been to survive Mary's suicide, I would never consider the path of suicide for myself. I wish Mary had felt worthy enough about herself to choose life, but I know from my own darkness that in my deepest despair, I didn't care if I lived or died. Seemingly like Mary, my own life didn't matter. It's mostly because of my husband, sons and friends that I choose life. And I would like to think that if Mary had known what her horrifying choice would do to her family and friends, she would not have ended her life.

Dark days still come and go. My healing has taken many years and is a slow process that I try to take one day at a time. One of my earliest stages of healing came in writing a letter to Mary six years after she died. It was part of an assignment for a psychology class.

March 3, 1983

Dear Mary,

I'm sitting here at Volunteer Park reflecting back to the time when you lived here. I moved back to Capitol Hill in September to return to college. At times I almost feel haunted as to your presence here. Your old apartments, Bonnie Watson's and The Roanoke St. Bridge are reminders of your troubled spirit.

All these years, almost six, I've felt a great deal of guilt about your suicide and wish so much I would be given another chance to relate with you. I'm taking a psychology class (my first one) and we were asked to write a letter concerning unfinished family business.

My tears are plentiful now. I can feel you here. The other day (2/28) I made a list of things I learned from your life, from you. I thought you'd like to know what they are. It sure is a better way to look at your life and you, instead of in the face of constant guilt and frustration.

I love you, I'll always love you. Not because you're my sister, but because of who you are. Look at what you've left me with.

First off, I learned that no words of wisdom can be received by someone who needs to be heard. What a great gift for you to leave me. Just think of all the people I have yet to encounter who need to be heard, rather than told. This makes me cry; it feels good. I'm listening now and this is the gift you're giving me right at this very moment.

Because of you, I've learned one has to go on with their life in spite of the loss of a loved one, in spite of the feeling of total failure, in spite of the life one feels responsible for.

I've allowed myself those guilt and failure feelings and am getting much better at coping. I'm growing and I continue to become stronger. I've learned that no matter how tough times get, not to give up. There's always a chance of a brighter day, a new road or a more joyous door.

I've found a few new roads this winter. The main one was to return to school to get my certificate so I feel more financially secure and so I can fulfill my desire to work with kids, not "just" as an aide. *The second door, which is still opening, is I've fallen in love, and it's an equal sharing relationship. I feel wonderful; so does he. Even Mom approves! I'll tell you more about him later. Now I want you to know what I've learned because of who you are.*

Although we weren't blood sisters, I realize you and I have a "learned behavior" bonding which will always keep us connected to one another. Sometimes I feel your suicide could've been a message to me that you needed to express in such a devastating manner in order to be heard, in order to make sure I would know you. All these years and I'm still shedding tears, still learning from your death and probably will spend a great deal of my own life putting the pieces of this puzzle together.

I've learned that looks don't matter. You were one of the prettiest women I've ever known. One of my housemates is much like you, Sagittarius no less! He's so gorgeous, yet he's screaming for people to see his inner beauty. I do and he's become like a brother to me. I told him in a letter on his birthday how much he reminded me of you and the inner beauty that's there, but that the outward beauty has its drawbacks.

And Tom, my new love, has looks much like mine, earthy, good, yet well worn and pock-marked. It doesn't matter. When we exchange our love, the shining we trigger in each other outweighs all else. It's wonderful. He's 3,000 miles away, so we have that dimension to deal with, hopefully not much longer— what a test of patience!

And you brought Maggie into this world—oh the beauty I see in that child. This really makes me cry my heart out. I wish so much you could see her, know her. Nothing but the finest. She's tall, thin, graceful, pretty and has a good sense of humor. She's sweet, generous, loving and strong. She's out of this world!

I feel you're fortunate to have had me here to relate with

her. Oh Mary, this makes me cry so hard, but I'm thankful,
too, because Maggie knows that one way she can connect with
you is through me. She comes to me, calls me and writes me
when she's in need. I'll be spending the summer in Buffalo and
she'll be 15—what a great time to interact closely with her. She
visited me out here last summer and I was back east at Christ-
mas—and there have been letters and tapes in between, so the
communication has been really good.

Just took a deep breath and feel really good about writing all
this. I'll write more later. Meanwhile, take good care of yourself
out there. I see you in others all the time. Your spirit lives on.
Much love always,
Lornie

∞

LONG AFTER Mom died, I heard a sermon by an Episcopal priest
that influenced my understanding of Mom's faith and how it affected me. In his sermon, the priest pointed out subtle ways in which
evangelism can make a difference. In one example, he referred to
evangelism as an infectious germ that could be received subcon-
sciously. The idea of Mom's faith being like an infectious germ was
astounding to me. Now I could counter-balance the germ which
Jane had spoken of, the negative germ my birth was for Mary.

I began looking at Mom's life in a whole new way, almost as
though I had inherited her faith. Mom's strength and determination
were revealed in the way she lived her own life. Her zest for life, her
sense of humor, and her strong Christian faith always pulled her
through. She would read her *Daily Word*, a Christian pamphlet of
daily meditations, and often share some of those meditations with
me. Mom was actively involved with the church and, as is common
with many parishioners, worshipped the clergy. In some providential

137

way, her introducing me to Tom, I believe, was her way of telling me I was and would be loved unconditionally forever. Although I don't attend church on a regular basis, the Christian faith has remained an important part of my spiritual journey. As with "my angels" from the prayer breakfasts in Stanwood, my prayer life has continued to be predominant in my ability to give thanks for the joyful things in my life. But in learning how to deal with my emotions, my faith didn't come as easily.

Mom and I always differed on how we dealt with our emotions. Mom never seemed to let her emotions get the best of her. It was as though she swooped them over her head and forgot they existed. Now I know she must've offered her problems to God, having faith that everything would work out all right. My emotions have always gotten the better of me, letting myself get overly attached to situations. With Mary, I would put myself in the middle of her problems, practically making them my own. For the longest time after she died, I couldn't distance myself from those problems and would become wrought up with feelings of responsibility. Part of it, I imagine, was because of my immaturity. But most of it, I believe, was because of my difficulty letting go. Mom always told me I was too analytical, not knowing how or when to put problems to rest. "Let go and let God," she would remind me.

In addition to Mom's constant reminding me to "not be so analytical," yoga practice has helped ease my internal dialogue. I took my first yoga class when I was in my late twenties. But it has taken umpteen more series of yoga classes over a couple of decades to remind me how important it is to slow down, breathe, center oneself and let go. I go in spurts, but for the most part I know if I don't do yoga regularly, I get overwhelmed with my life. At that point, I'm no good to anyone, similar to how I was in trying to rescue Mary.

My foremost passion, gardening, has also been one of my greatest teachers. There's a true deepening of my soul when I dig my hands into the earth and tend to the life of my plants. From the days of the Mother Earth Plant Shop and my first vegetable garden, to some of my more sophisticated landscaping, I have come to realize how emotionally therapeutic gardening can be. Just as I have had trouble letting go of old messages I replay in my head, it takes a long time for me to toss hopelessly dying plants that I've nurtured for a long time. The beauty which is revealed once I weed out the old plants, is similar to the calm I feel when I detach myself from feeling unrealistic responsibility. Morrie Schwartz' wisdom in the book *Tuesdays with Morrie,* by Mitch Albom, has reinforced my ability of letting go. In his life journey, he learned to feel the pain when it surfaced, and then let go, knowing it would return and could be dealt with again later.

I used to think it was solely my inner strength and courage that made me determined to overcome my dark days. Now I know that Mom made a lasting impression on my long struggles with insecurities and depression. Continually reminding myself of Mom's ability to cope with hardships and live life fully, I have embraced her infectious faith germ, letting go of the "if onlys" and forgiving myself for the years of not finding peace with Mary and for feeling like the negative germ in her life. Through growing up with Mom's spirituality, years of therapy, my own inner strength and courage, practicing yoga, gardening, and the sheer determination not to end up like Dad or Mary, I have learned to forgive Mary, Dad, and, most importantly, myself.

SEVENTEEN

He Knew

THE CLOUDS had temporarily lifted late that morning when I picked up Dad and headed to Thunder Bay. Lobo was to join us later. The car ride was awkward. It remained quiet except for some of my usual small talk. My anxiety was increasing about talking to Dad. I wanted to finally talk about leaving the east coast, but wasn't quite ready. I yearned for him to share some heart-to-heart sadness with me, but it seemed I was looking for the impossible. I never saw Dad cry over Mary's death, and I've seen only a couple spells of tears since Mom's absence. He seems to tuck it way down deep.

I approached Dad during lunch. Taking a few deep breaths, I decided it was now or never. "Dad, the hardest thing for me in leaving again is having to say good-bye to you." I was looking straight at him.

With his head turned, not looking at me at all, he mumbled, "Yeah, but we agreed to visit each other once a year," and he hummed that god-awful hum that I've heard so many times before. Oh God,

I don't know why I expected more. It can't end like this, I thought. It just can't. I remembered the last time I heard that hum, the hum without words that says, "Oh, what a merry day it is; I see only the road in front of me." It was the summer following Mom's death, the summer of '91. I was forty-one. Dad and I were driving into Buffalo from Thunder Bay. Again I had been fishing for emotional support. Don't I ever learn. I told him that the preceding year had been the hardest year of my life.

I elaborated, beginning with my teaching year. "This past year's class has been hell to deal with. I've had no time to absorb Mom's death or give Jamie and Alex the attention they deserve."

And there was that hum. I remember driving down Porter Avenue, thinking, here I am in mid-life, having just experienced an exceedingly hard year, and all I get is that HUM. I wanted to kill him.

I took a deep breath and tried to return to our lunch conversation. I acknowledged our agreement to visit each other once a year, and fell silent, wondering if we would ever connect.

∞

MAGGIE AND Lobo arrived close to the same time, after my chance to talk with Dad had failed. Lobo drove up first. With a sigh of relief, I welcomed him, knowing that the silence would be broken. The pain of rejection would subside and we could go on with the day as planned.

"Anyone up for a swim?" Lobo asked cheerfully. Dad hadn't gone down to the beach in over a year; the stairs were too much for him.

"Let me finish cleaning up from lunch, then I'll join you," I responded.

Swimming with Lobo had become our chance to share our

frustrations about Dad. But that day, our swim never happened. I watched Lobo proceed with his routine. Whether or not he had already eaten upon his arrival, the first thing he always did was open the fridge. Then he checked the canned goods. I watched as he pulled out a saucepan, heated up some Chef Boy-R-Dee and added all his hot sauces. Yuk! Dad was waiting for dessert. Oh God, I thought, I had forgotten lunchtime dessert! Fortunately, I found a box of Oreos in the cupboard which sufficed.

Like the wind, Maggie threw open the screen door and entered with her usual flare. "Hi, everybody!" Her warm smile could melt anyone.

She greeted Lobo, hugged me and went over to Dad, giving him a huge hug and kiss. Breaking away from the kiss, she looked down at Dad. "Hi, Bomps, how's it going?"

Dad smiled, loving to be kissed. "I'm fine, how about for you?"

"I'm doing great." Maggie was excited. "In fact, if it's all right with you, I'm going to Bosma's (our local gardening center) to get some plants for the front of the house."

Lobo interrupted. "Don't go to Bosma's. Isabel will be arriving with a surprise later."

Taking a deep breath, "what kind of surprise?" Maggie pursued. She'd already had one too many of Isabel's surprises. Without giving Lobo a chance to respond "I want to go to Bosma's NOW." The clouds were threatening again and I presumed Maggie wanted to get things planted in case the rain came.

Hesitantly, not one for conflicts, Lobo gave way to share a portion of Isabel's surprise. "Isabel has some plants she started on her own and wants to give them to us."

"Just tell me what kind of plants, and I'll get other ones," Maggie went on.

"It's supposed to be a surprise." Lobo was getting angry. "I'm not going to spoil it for her."

"I'm tired of Isabel's surprises." Maggie was fuming. "She's already changed the spices, put new bedspreads in my bedroom, added her painting to the wall, and Lornie tells me she even had a luncheon here last week for her own friends."

Lobo was quick to defend. "Dad said it was OK for her to have her friends here."

Still fuming, Maggie dragged me into it. "Lornie, don't you agree Isabel acts as though she owns this place?"

I was standing by the screen door getting ready to go wash off the chairs on the back porch while Lobo was eating. All I really wanted to do was go for a swim and reconstruct my plan of attack with Dad.

Maggie knew I agreed; now I had to confess it. "Yeah, there have been a lot of changes around here because of Isabel."

Lobo is not one to anger quickly, but he needed to defend his lover, the woman who was giving him purpose in life, the woman who had brought him alive, kept the beach house alive. He marched out of the kitchen area, walked over to the huge picture windows overlooking Lake Erie and put his hands on his hips. "*I* bought the spices, *I* bought the picture for the wall. Isabel's helping ME. Get mad at me if you want, but don't blame Isabel."

But Maggie and Isabel had never warmed up to each other and Maggie certainly wasn't going to back down now. "Then why does SHE entertain her friends for lunch without any of our family being here?" Maggie was convinced she had Lobo cornered.

I watched as Lobo's body seemed to overpower Maggie who had sat down at the dining room table, daring him to defend Isabel over family.

He continued his defense. "For your information, Isabel and some of her friends came here a couple of weekends ago with me to get this place cleaned up and ready for Lornie's visit and the summer months ahead. She asked me if she could reward them by having them here for lunch this past week. Dad said it was OK."

Making sure she wasn't alone, Maggie called me back into the middle. "Come on, Lornie, just this morning you said to me you were tired of Isabel acting as though she owns this place."

A deep breath followed as I knew this was a no-win battle. "Maggie's right, Lobo." I tried to be gentle. "And especially this plant business bothers me. When we moved to Syracuse last year, I remember being excited that I would be close enough to participate in the yard work here, as well as helping Dad open the house for the summer. It seems like a lot of decisions are being made without all of us in mind."

"For crying out loud," Lobo said in disbelief. "You're about to move to Washington. You can't help out here."

Feeling defensive, I continued my plea. "I may not be able to help in the future, but that doesn't negate what I can do now." I should have stopped then, but I was on a roll. "Come on, Lobo, admit it. Isabel has made a bunch of changes, some of which I don't feel are fair."

Dad was gritting his teeth. He witnessed this whole fiasco from his chair on the front porch. The enclosed front porch, with two huge glass doors, opens from the spacious living area. His face was red and I'm sure his blood pressure was off the charts. Lobo was finally happy with his life. And Isabel was the main reason for his happiness. I'm sure Dad didn't want to spoil that. I didn't either.

But Isabel wasn't just coming between me and Lobo, she was coming between me and Dad. Every time I turned around, Dad was praising Isabel. "Isabel gave me chocolates for Easter." "Isabel did such a great job cleaning out the kitchen." "Isabel knows how to sew bedspreads." Isabel, Isabel, Isabel. I was sick of hearing her name. Sick of hearing that she knew how to do everything.

Lobo was running out of steam. We all paused for a moment.

Then Dad spoke up. "Why don't you talk this over with Isabel once she arrives? It doesn't seem fair when Isabel isn't here to speak for herself." I was impressed with Dad's levelheadedness and, although he was right, I hated to think of Isabel defending herself. She had a law degree and was no slouch.

We agreed to cool off. Even Maggie said she'd wait for Isabel's plants before going to Bosma's.

Lobo didn't want to look at me, much less take a swim together. He putzed around the kitchen while I washed the porch chairs and Maggie began weeding. Dad was still reading the morning paper. Either he read it very thoroughly, or snoozed more than he admitted! I invited him to join me out back where the sun had broken through and its warmth felt inspiring. The freshened terrace chairs awaited company.

I grabbed a magazine and sat opposite Dad, thinking of how Mom used to take advantage of the midday sun on this terrace. Thinking of how it was Dad and I who built this terrace. I had loved being his carpenter's helper. I looked around at the cement blocks that thirty years before we had laid so carefully. It was on this very terrace that I learned how to use a level. Before laying each cement block, we had to smooth out the sand, shoveling out any excess, so that the new block would be level with the block which preceded it. We used a large, four-foot level to find the exactness for which Dad hoped.

As I gazed at Dad sitting in that old, green metal chair, I could visualize Mom sitting alongside him in the matching chair in which I was now perched. Mom was gone and there would never be another chance for me to feel the connectedness with her for which I longed. I wanted it so badly from Dad. I wanted to feel as important as Mary, as important as Lobo had become. I needed to be his special little girl. I was thinking to myself "Here I am, Dad. Do you see me?" I was screaming inside for his love. I couldn't bear the pain and started to cry.

Lobo had come out to the terrace to clean the grill behind us and was heading back indoors when I pulled my chair closer to Dad's, put my hand on his knee and told him I was hurting. I think Lobo knew something was happening, and I wasn't sure if he stayed in earshot after letting the screen door close behind him.

It all came out. "Dad, I'm sorry for all the arguing this afternoon. But it's true. Ever since Isabel came into the picture, it's as though I don't even exist. You're always praising Lobo and Isabel. I feel I don't belong here. I feel like I'm not part of the family anymore. It's as though Isabel has taken Mom's place and no one cares about Mom anymore." I couldn't stop. "And then when we were out on the porch having lunch, I tried to tell you how hard it is for me to leave again and you couldn't even look at me."

He started to cry. Dad was crying. We were both crying. I leaned over to hug him and felt the baby soft skin of his face against mine, like two babies needing to be needed.

"Lornie, I love you so much." There, he said it. I wasn't sure if I really heard any more. He told me he loved me. He said it with tears, with his heart. He cared beyond doubt. The rest was background music. "I didn't know you were feeling this way. Of course you belong in the family. Of course I'm going to miss you terribly." He wasn't choking anymore. He had straightened up and told me how much he missed Mom. "No one could ever take her place," he said with all his heart.

Affirming his love, I thanked him and reiterated my heartfelt love. "I love you too, Daddy. It kills me to have to leave you, but I love the West. I must go." I didn't need to tell him that it was the West where I belonged. He knew.

ABOUT THE AUTHOR

LORNIE WALKER was born in Buffalo, NY in 1950. She has been a freelance writer of human interest stories for small-town newspapers for over 20 years. With a BA in Special Education and Psychology, Walker has taught kindergarten, works with the elderly and mentors children with special needs. She also manages a retreat cottage on one of Puget Sound's magnificent islands while tending her gardens. She lives in Washington State with her husband and two sons.

ISBN 141208573-X